KALEIDOSCOPE

NOTTINGHAMSHIRE

Edited by Sarah Lester

First published in Great Britain in 1999 by
POETRY NOW YOUNG WRITERS
Remus House,
Coltsfoot Drive,
Woodston,
Peterborough, PE2 9JX
Telephone (01733) 890066

HB ISBN 0 75430 383 7
SB ISBN 0 75430 384 5

FOREWORD

This year, the Poetry Now Young Writers' Kaleidoscope competition proudly presents the best poetic contributions from over 32,000 up-and-coming writers nationwide.

Successful in continuing our aim of promoting writing and creativity in children, each regional anthology displays the inventive and original writing talents of 11-18 year old poets. Imaginative, thoughtful, often humorous, *Kaleidoscope Nottinghamshire* provides a captivating insight into the issues and opinions important to today's young generation.

The task of editing inevitably proved challenging, but was nevertheless enjoyable thanks to the quality of entries received. The thought, effort and hard work put into each poem impressed and inspired us all. We hope you are as pleased as we are with the final result and that you continue to enjoy *Kaleidoscope Nottinghamshire* for years to come.

CONTENTS

Sam Chambers	65
Alexa Marsh	66
Rebecca Walker	66
Sarah Hughes	67
Leighann Bell	67
Stephanie Harrison	68
Lacey Redford	68
Rebecca Osborn	69
Rosie Edson	69
Michelle Hancock	70
Claire Foulds	70
Jennifer Longden	71
Lisa Kirk	71
Peter Sowerbutts	72
Sarah Garnett	72
Megan Levi Bird	73
Sarah Pryor	73
Thomas Elliott	74
Mark J Carnall	74
Benjamin Matthews	75
Hayley M Boswell	76
Daniel Murphy	76
Kerry Brewer	77
Victoria Prest	78
Tom Renshaw	79
Simon Chambers	80
Gemma Crossland	80
Vanessa Dobson	81
Robert Freeman	81
Rhys Bethell	82
Ian Dickson	82
Gemma Jones	83
Ryan Willows	83
Dean Walker	84
Emma Footitt	84
Scott Marshall	85
Lucy Walker	85
Gavin Keogh	86

James Homer	86
Rebecca Allen	87
Laura Taylor	87
Kerri Sian Lilliman	88
Natalie Hudspeth	88
Megan Geach	89
Christopher Hart	90
Thomas Spurden	90
Emily Pilsworth	91
Katherine Garton	92
Robert Walker	92
John Bowmer	93
Kayleigh Skelding	94
Sasha Summers	94
Crystal Wilkinson	95
James Mason	96

Kirkby Centre School

Craig Swinton	96
Johanna Beasley	97
Adam Leake	97
Ian Hughes	98
Marie Louise Hand	99
Rebecca Patrick	100
Joanne Ward	101
Daniel Linfield	102
Gareth Hill	102
Amy Peat	103
Nicky Kiddy	103
Wayne Skermer	104
Nicola Payne	104
Ryan Greensmith	105
Kelly Bradbury	105
Adam Hinds	106
David Barnes	106
Amy Smith	107
Matthew Ward	107
Blake Evans	107

Stephanie Reynolds	108
Stephen Morgan	109
Stephanie Scothern	110
Lee Turner	110
Victoria Cottam	111
Adam Bramley	111
Samantha Utting	112
Karley Otter	112
Sarah Scothern	113
Robert Saunders	113
Matthew Rawding	114
Paul Cresswell	114
Neil Whysall	115

Rodney School

David Dewberry	115
Abigail Gull	116
Rainbow Ho	117
Lynsey Stapleford	118
Briony Conduit	119
Jordan Miller	120
Daniel Shieber	121
Chris Formon	121
Katie Shieber	122
Jonathan Siddons	122
Kieran Green	123
Francis Tam	123
Sophie Frost	124
Martin Turner	124
Darren Rumfitt	125
Lance Leivers	125

Windmill Ridge Middle School

Natalie Shaw	126
Frankie Bean	127
Joe Forman	127
Lewis Garrington	128
Ryan Williams	128

The Poems

I Am Lost

I am lost
Lost in an endless dream,
Of pain and everlasting heat
I can never seem to wake from this dream
In my dream I run,
I don't know to where or when I'll stop.
I am lost in an endless dream,
I am lost in the dream without you.
I run to seek shelter
Shelter from pain and hurt and loneliness.
I feel sad and out of control of life
And run to try and lose all life's challenges
I wake in floods of tears to find you're not next to me
I break into a sweat as the pain hits me.
It hits me like a thousand knives stabbing into me one at a time
It will be the same tomorrow night
Unless you're beside me as I wake.

Jemma Wakeley

Scream

Hallowe'en! Hallowe'en!
It's enough to make you scream
With witches on broomsticks
That fly through the sky
Skeletons and ghosts which lurk around
It's enough to make you scream
Pumpkins that flicker and glow
On every window-sill
Children all dressed up and ready to go
Hallowe'en! Hallowe'en!

Thomas Fazackerley (11)
Belvoir High School

GREY

What is a stormy cloud
And hair whitened by age?
A fluffy grey rabbit
The gloomy early morning light
Whitened from darkness?
A gravestone
A can from a drink machine
Sorrow and dismay?
The dullest colour
Is grey.

What is a tabloid newspaper
And a ghost in your room
A morning of fog
An afternoon of rain?
The number 10 gate
The house key in your purse
Light stones on a snowman's head
A seagull in a field?
The dullest colour
Is grey.

What is that granite on the path
And weathervane above your church
And a squirrel from that tree?
The shadow of you
Slowly fading from the night
The second place medal
The second place cup
The unknown dullness?
The dullest colour
Is grey.

Louise Tinsley (13)
Belvoir High School

WHY GREEN?

Why green?
The crocodile or the frog.

Why green?
The moss upon the log,
For the plants and evergreen trees.

Why green?
To calm, to please?
The lettuce or the cabbage,
Flowers, lily pads and the grass.

Why green?
The jade of the sea or lake,
The juicy apple or the pear,
The scaly skin of a hissing snake.

Why green?
The fairytale dragon in its lair,
The pure green eyes of every cat,
Why this 'green' for these things?

It's the colour of life and that's that!

Zoe Tomaszewski
Belvoir High School

CHOCOLATE

I'm in a sea of ice-cream
So boring, white and plain
Now I've eaten all the chocolate
It'll never be the same.

Alice Munks (10)
Belvoir High School

SPORT'S MY GAME

Racing, dancing,
No time for romancing.
Always dancing,
I like sky-diving.
Sport's my game,
Adam's my name.
Hockey makes me act like a monkey
And untied shoes make me feel darey.
Tennis makes me worn out
Too worn out.
I need to sit down before I go dizzy.

Adam Roper (10)
Belvoir High School

WHAT I MEAN TO YOU

I'm the rabbit in the headlights
I'm the gum stuck on your shoe
I'm the tower you're destroying
Is this what I mean to you?

I'm the water that keeps dripping
I'm the homework you must do
I'm the record that is broken
Is this what I mean to you?

I'm the angel with black wings
I'm the dying bird that sings
To you I don't mean anything
I'm just there . . .

Lucy Chell-Munks (13)
Belvoir High School

HALLOWE'EN

October 31st the evening was drawing nigh,
Children in the street and a full moon graced the sky.
Excitedly I ran home to get my costume on,
A witch I was to be, the cat ones had all gone.
The Jack-o-lantern was aglow as I ran up to the door,
Everything was in darkness, I felt a bit unsure.
The door creaked open eerily as I called out to my mum,
But nothing stirred inside the house, I wanted to turn and run.
I summoned up the courage and stepped into the room,
I reached out for the light switch to shed some light on all the gloom.
My attention was attracted towards the windowpane,
When I heard a 'tap tap tapping', and someone whispering my name.
I tippy-toed across the room as quiet as a mouse,
I could've sworn I was alone in the dark and eerie house.
I tightly gripped the window ledge and swung it open wide,
A thick white mist was all around, and swirling blew inside.
I rubbed my eyes and squinted but still I couldn't see,
Then two long bony arms reached in and boomed
            'Now come with me!'

Samantha Kamani (11)
Belvoir High School

THE RIVER

Tumbling and falling,
Down an everlasting stream of life,
Spraying its white beads,
Like pearls from a watery heaven,
Crashing against the rocks,
Like thunder in a storm,
In the quiet eddies,
Beavers building dams,
Out of a forest of golden leaves.

Jenny Fox (10)
Belvoir High School

AFTERMATH

The grey swirl of ashes fills the air.
Eyes glare, people leave, others come.
Panic fills the now traumatised street.
The smell of hot ashes sears the noses of all involved.
Fear.
Threat.
Haste.
The flame brings down everything that gets in its way,
like a bulldozer on a mission.
Heat puts colour to the cheeks of the palest onlookers.
Leaves sizzle in the heat, and smoke smears any object still standing.
Flashing blue lights can be seen in the distance.
The sound of the sirens can almost be heard above the
crackling of the blaze.
Are they too late,
or will they make it in time to save the helpless victim
stranded amongst her burned and singed possessions?

Hayley Jenkins (18)
Elizabethan High School

THE WRITER OF THIS POEM

The writer of this poem,
Is as tall as a giraffe,
As smooth as a Labrador,
Lying in the grass.

As cuddly as a teddy,
Lying on a bed.
Has a jam-packed imagination,
Stored inside her head.

She's as bright as the sun,
As sharp as a knife.
As slick as a tiger,
That pounces in a trice.

She's as strong as a bear,
As beautiful as a rose.
As bold as a lion,
But as warm as a stove.

As lively as an ant,
As busy as a bee.
Set me a challenge,
And see the real me.

As loud as a trumpet,
Blaring its merry tune.
You will hear me coming,
Even if you're in the next room.

As stylish as a peacock,
Fanning out its tail.
As cool as the snow,
I'm determined not to fail.

Laura A Hopkins (11)
Elizabethan High School

HAVE A NICE DAY!

Hordes of people swarm round the smooth polished counter.
Yells of orders fly through the air;
Over the accumulating din
The spitting and hissing of French fries can be heard
As they sizzle and fry in the seething oil.

Families deploy - seats have to be found!
Frantic waves as they reunite with food.
Appealing odours drift from the vast selection -
Deluxe, mega-deluxe, mega-meals.
Serviettes and straws? Any sauces or sugar?
The choices alone startle a newcomer.

Like bullets from a gun
The packed, polystyrene boxes
Shoot down the silvery slopes
To be exchanged for cash:
A deal has been done.

Children sit with their fresh toys
Firmly glued to their hands.
Smiley workers with stripy hats
Wander around waving flags,
While balloons are moored to their arms.

The food's eaten; the people go
Just leaving
Their empty cartons
Lying around . . .
That's all there is to show.

Amy Davy (17)
Elizabethan High School

8

FIELD OF REMEMBRANCE

I grasp the poppy in my hands,
The petals dark as blood,
Remembering a time when soldiers
Fought and died upon this mud.

My poppy, and a thousand more,
Waver in the breeze,
Memories of a nation lost,
For a land they tried to please.

Each petal is a feeling,
That touched the soldiers' hearts;
The desperate fear and sadness
As they saw all hope depart.

The green stem is the new life
That they wanted to achieve
And the centre is the memory
That was all they had to leave.

The gentle rustle of the wind
Was then artillery roar,
And the sweet scent of the grass
Was the stench of blood and gore,

In a field where war has savaged strong,
And men gave in to hate,
Where morals were forgotten,
And forgiveness came too late.

Claire Lacy-Jones (15)
Elizabethan High School

THE WRITER OF THIS POEM

The writer of this poem
is smaller than a mouse,
as curious as a Labrador dog
and frightened by a woodlouse!

As delicate as a jeweller
with my grandma's china pots,
as cheeky and mischievous
as naughty little tots.

As clever as a professor
I'm joking can't you tell,
as helpful as a doctor
when you don't feel too well.

As kind as an angel
as gorgeous as one too!
As loyal and as trusting
the dearest friend to you.

As funny as a comedian
a bunch of laughs is all I am,
as surprising as a magician
but as gentle as a lamb.

The writer of this poem
is quite shy you can see,
so let's keep this poem
a secret between you and me.

Rachael Smith (11)
Elizabethan High School

THE HIGH DIVE

I see water, people
swimming,
The ripples splashing on
the side.

I hear people shouting
and
splashing.

I smell the funny smell
you only
smell in the swimming
baths

I feel the water slap
against
me as I hit the rippled
water
slap!

I taste the horrible
taste
of chlorine
yuck!

James Denman (11)
Elizabethan High School

A Day In The Life Of A Soldier In The Trenches

Watching, waiting,
For the piercing sounds of the whistle
For the commanding bawl of 'over the top'
For the prickling on my skin like a thistle
To just fade away and to stop.

Shouting, screaming,
At the deafening noise of explosions
At the pain and torture you feel
At yourself to control your emotions
Oh why is this hell so real?

Moaning, groaning,
Because the gas mask did not fit you; why?
Because your lungs are corrupted with smoke
Because you know you are going to die
Folk laugh but it is not a joke.

Dying, flying,
You float above to those great golden gates
You fly to a garden of pink and blue
You can forget all your troubles and hates
And someone is there to greet you.

Sophie Priestley (15)
Elizabethan High School

Torturers, Torturers

I see torturers advancing towards me, with axes in their hands.
I hear the torturers' cruel laughter filling my ears.
I taste blood on my lips from the last person who was tortured.
I smell the musty odour of the stinking torture chamber.
I feel panic-stricken; I want to get it over with.

Thomas Bennett (11)
Elizabethan High School

THE FIGHT

His fist makes contact,
His opponent goes down,
He dances 'round the ring like a triumphant stag.

The atmosphere is electric,
The crowd are hushed,
His opponent is lying lifeless on the canvas.

The ring groans under the strain,
His opponent heaves himself over,
Sitting up, slowly, standing.

The 'ping' of the bell means the end of the round,
As they touch gloves, the silence is shattered,
And a sigh of relief is expelled by all.

The bell goes again,
In for round two,
Adrenaline pumps as fists crack together.

The final bell rings,
The decision is made,
A good time for all and the night is over.

Rebecca Limb (18)
Elizabethan High School

AT HOME

I see a green cosy chair, all covered in cotton.
I hear the TV muttering along in the background
of a programme.
I smell the air freshener swifting round the room.
I taste scrumptious chocolate while watching the TV.
I feel a really good book in my hands.

Kylie Maule (11)
Elizabethan High School

THE FIRE

The fire is a clashing beast,
With his jaws wide open and giving off heat
His long claws about two feet,
And his roar as loud as the sea.

He is mad and angry,
His brain set on having a feast,
He has caught it now his prey,
He is eating it now piece by piece,
The fire is a roaring beast.

He is sometimes calm,
And sometimes sleeps,
But once he has got going,
It is hard to keep,
Him silent and still and not a peep,
The fire is a big mad beast.

Once he is quiet,
He will now rest,
Now he isn't making a mess,
The fire is a sleeping beast.

Simon Wilkinson (13)
Elizabethan High School

THE NIGHT I SAT ON THE QUIET BEACH

I see the waves crashing against the rocks,
I see the waves crashing against the wall.
I hear the seagulls squealing,
I taste the seafood.
I feel the smooth sandy sand
And I feel the smooth seashells.

Stacey Bryce (11)
Elizabethan High School

WINTER

White soft flakes of snow fall,
Onto the emerald green grass.
The crystal clear ice covers rivers,
And snow piles up in a great white mass.

The icy flakes twirl and swirl,
Floating in the current of the air.
Animals hibernate in the winter,
Waiting for spring in their lair.

The cold wind blows the soft flakes about,
Its icy chill gives frostbite.
People wrap up warm in coats,
Especially at night.

All the snow settles down,
On the bare and frosty ground.
Floating down like a feather,
And not making a single sound.

Matthew Ingman (11)
Elizabethan High School

ON THE ISLE OF WIGHT

I see boats and ferries crossing and the waves breaking up.
I hear the foghorns of the boats and the waves crashing against
the breakwaters.
I smell the fish and the sea's pleasant smell.
I taste fish in my mouth and chips frying from the local
chip shop.
I feel sharp rocks on my feet and the sea breezes in my hair.

Chris Searson (11)
Elizabethan High School

THE WRITER OF THIS POEM

The writer of this poem
Is as quick as a snail
Is as strong as a mouse
And is as fit as Michael Flatley.

I am as cuddly as a fluffy kitten
As clean as clear water
As tidy as can be
And as small as a newly planted tree.

I am as clever as all the people in the world put together
I am as neat as the richest man on earth
I'm as bright as a fresh flower
And I smell as fresh as a rose.

I am as gorgeous as a puppy
As mischievous as an evil wizard
As colourful as a rainbow
As innocent as a tiny baby.

Francesca Civitillo (11)
Elizabethan High School

AT BEDTIME

I see my blazing gas fire in front of me
spreading its warmth.
I hear the continuous tick tock tick tock
from our clock on the light pink wall.
I smell the hot chocolate my dad is making.
I taste the chocolate that burns my tongue
I feel the fluffy white rug I'm sat upon.

Lee Scott (12)
Elizabethan High School

BEING BORN

Confronted with my landlord at last,
Nine months of patient waiting ended
No longer a lodger in that building
But in the weird ways of the world.

Against my will, I have been evicted;
Pushed and punched, like a boxer in the ring
Forced from the soft heated chamber
Into the harsh white coldness of the labour room.

Bangs, clicks and whirrs probe my ears
While faces look down at me.
My landlord seems proud
Now that she has stopped screaming.

The pale man, who was next to her
Now has colour in his cheeks;
Grasped snugly, against warm flesh
It all seems worth it, now.

Layla Slade (17)
Elizabethan High School

NOT THE NINE O'CLOCK NEWS

I see the fuzzy and tedious television when on comes
the six o'clock news.

I hear my mum cooking dinner, rattling the saucepans
and the tap spitting out water.

I smell bacon, egg and mushrooms sizzling in the hot pan.

I feel the cold and smooth TV remote in my hand.

Oliver Hill (11)
Elizabethan High School

CHRISTMAS SHOPPING IN THE CITY

Busy shoppers in busy streets,
trotting by on tiring feet.
On a never-ending raid,
to make it to the shopping arcade.

The temperature's rising, as off you go,
pushchair, handbag and husband in tow.
This roundabout for shoppers is driving you mad,
and you can't get your head around what to get Dad.

Wading crowds like a fast flowing stream,
not stopping to admire displays as they gleam.
Toddlers screaming as Mum walks too fast,
and the toys in the windows go shooting past.

Jolly songs and Christmas lights,
festive joy at dizzy heights.
All the stress is part of the fun,
The silly season has begun.

Suzannah Bedford (17)
Elizabethan High School

THE SEA

The huge waves crashing against the rugged rocks,
The spray smacking me in the face as the waves come in.
Like a patron of the sea protecting others,
They destroy anything in their path they want to like a giant.
The waves themselves sound like a stick hitting a cymbal,
The waves gleam at people on the beach.
Whining on every calm day,
Promising eternal protection and forgiveness always.

Scott Mableson (13)
Elizabethan High School

FIRE

Fire is the living demon on earth
ruler of death and hell on earth.
Fire is the red flame of hell,
devil's one and only true pal
Fire is the sun so burning and
hot.
Fire is a burning session of passion
Fire is red, red is stop, danger
ahead.
Fire is like the devil's anger
Fire is like a roaring lion in the
jungle.
A flicking light that lights my
life.

Luci Rolfe (13)
Elizabethan High School

ME

The writer of this poem is as tall as a pencil,
Is as good as David Beckham,
As brave as Hercules,
As cool as a winter's breeze,
With eyes like an owl.
As clever as Einstein,
With a body like Prince Nazim,
As stylish as a fashion show,
The writer of this poem is . . .
Me, of course.

Dougie McMaster (11)
Elizabethan High School

SURFING

I see the waves crashing up the sand,
biting the sand apart with its jaws.

I hear the cry of seagulls and wind whistling
out over the sea.

I smell the cold sea air and the strong smell
of wax on my surfboard.

I taste the fresh salty sea air, it sticks in the
back of my throat.

I feel the freezing cold water running over my
feet and the sharp wind blowing through my hair . . .

Paul Bullock (12)
Elizabethan High School

MY NAN AND GRANDAD

My nan is not very old
She tells me to do what I am told
She gives me money
Her family are not very funny

My grandad is not very old
He is grand
He gives me a hand
In my topics at school
I think he is cool!

Helen Newton (11)
Elizabethan High School

SEASIDE

I see the golden sand, the crashing dark
blue waves and the children playing.

I hear a boat speeding along the water
and the children shouting happily.

I smell the salty sea and the fish and chips.

I taste the salt and vinegar covered
fish and chips.

I feel the soft velvety sand trickling through
my toes.

Adrienne Chessman (11)
Elizabethan High School

FIRE

Fire is like a guardian of death,
It roars like thunder, its jaws like a sauna.
It eats any building, falling, crashing.
It fears all water steals all life,
Fire has a destiny, its father the sun.

Fire is a dreadnought a reminder of hell,
A being of surprises a species we don't know.
It eats up souls, scares our body,
Fire is a reminder, a reminder of hell.

Martyn Smith (13)
Elizabethan High School

THE GOLDEN PAW

There's a cat that lives next door,
Who's coal-black and fluffy,
Apart from his one golden paw,
Which is sparkling and lovely.

In the very middle of the night,
He silently creeps around the garden,
Then in the morning when it's light,
You can see where his paws have fallen.

For in each place his golden toes fell,
There stood a glistening blue bell.

Rose Shepherd (11)
Elizabethan High School

MYSTERIOUS NIGHT

I see the planets, the stars, the moon, the sun
and the Milky Way sprout eyes and mouths
as I look up into the dark sky.
I hear them talking to each other with loud,
thunderous voices.
I smell the night's dew, cold and fresh,
I taste the cold icy rainfall falling down from
the dark sky,
I feel the rain, I'm cold, as it pours down to the ground
from the mysterious sky.

Stephanie Sunley (11)
Elizabethan High School

WARTIME

I hear the sound of cannons and drums
as I curl up in my bottomless trench.
I smell my dirt-covered uniform and the strong
smell of gunpowder.
I see the fire blaze across the battlefield
and planes fly slowly over me.
I taste cold steel as I pull the pin
Of a bright green grenade
and taste of soil as it blows into my face.
I feel a sharp pain in my back as I fall to the ground:
I feel a sheet being pulled over me.

Kieron J Lacey
Elizabethan High School

RAIN

Rain is wet, dull and heavy,
Rain comes before thunder and lightning.
Too much rain brings disaster,
Rivers rip raw and there is water everywhere.
If it is not too heavy,
Rain brings puddles.
If you do not wear your raincoat
And wellies or use an umbrella,
You have to stay inside,
Looking up at the black clouds in the sky.

Laura Shaw (13)
Elizabethan High School

ALIEN SISTER

When angry her eyes pop out,
her skin goes purple and bumpy.
If she really wants something
and you don't let her have it,
her arms get longer.
On the end of her nails are long teeth
starting to grow.
Then she grabs you and tries to put holes
in you with her nails.
Tries to scoff herself at mealtimes,
then burps loudly.
(Better hold on, or you will blow away)
Blows your head off,
when making a sound
to try and distract her from her homework,
if she has done something wrong,
then she fabricates.
Needs someone strong to keep her under control.
Favourite food - everything she sees.

Natalie Jeffery (13)
King Edward VI School

FRIENDS

Friends will always care
They'll always be around
They'll try to cheer you up
If you're feeling bad or down.

Friends will keep your secrets
With them, things are fun
Even if you've lost the race
With friends you'll think you've won.

Sometimes you'll fall out
Close mates usually do
But you'll make up just as soon
Good friends do that too.

You can't buy friends with money
It doesn't work that way
Those friends will just desert you
Real friends are here to stay.

Kate Elliott (13)
King Edward VI School

THE SCHOOL BULLY

He is always in the ring,
With his fists up high.
Punching the lights out of her or him.
He is getting into more and more trouble now,
I wish it would stop.
It will end in tears
I know it will.
He will go to prison
All because of his fists,
All because he was the school bully.
One of these days he will go too far,
He will push someone to the ground
And they will not get up
And all because of his fists.
The day may come when he is picked on
And then and only then he will know what it feels
Like to be picked on.

Katie Davies (12)
King Edward VI School

SCHOOL'S A NIGHTMARE

My first day at school
Was such a tragic day
I got bullied, lost my books
And couldn't find my way
The chips just taste like cardboard
And always are so cold
The sausage rolls are soggy
And they are full of mould
The maths teacher's a monster
And science is so dull
My teacher for geography
Is like a raging bull.

Ryan Draper (13)
King Edward VI School

FLYING PIGS

I often wondered if pigs could really fly,
it would be a funny sight to see them up high in the sky.
Just imagine them with wings,
bobbing up and down like springs.
They could have parties high up there,
or there might even be a fair.
I read about flying pigs in a book,
but there never is any when you look.
When I think of it, if pigs could fly,
the price of bacon would be sky high.

Charlotte Longden (13)
King Edward VI School

A JOURNEY UNKNOWN

'The last mission in life is death',
Is the phrase that echoes around my head,
As I feel my soul slip from my body.
My head is spinning as all the secrets of life
            are revealed,
My life was fulfilled,
My life was exhausted,
I think of all the things I've done
As I slowly rise high.
Soon I am soaring,
To a place where I feel relaxed, carefree,
Where I know I can rest in the protection of
            Him, the Morning Star.

Rachael Smith (13)
King Edward VI School

I DREAM

I dream that one day I'll grow fins and a tail,
I'd see the world's oceans,
And not once have to sail.

I'd go where I liked, I would just have to swim,
If I chose who I was I would be a dolphin.

If I was a shark I would explore the coral reef
I'd scare people off by showing them my teeth.

But I supposed I'd get bored of sea and soggy sand,
In the end I think I'll stay on dry land.

Victoria Atkinson (14)
King Edward VI School

MY BROTHER, THE PAIN!

My brother is starting at our school today,
Oh no it's a disaster!
I dread to think what he will do,
Please don't electrocute the headmaster!

It's time to wait for the bus,
He's already acting up.
He's acting rather daft,
Squealing and screeching and yapping like a pup!

Here is the part I'm dreading,
The bus stop after school.
There he is amongst the crowd,
He's doing it again, he thinks he is really cool!

He's doing his best impression of a crow,
They all think he is insane.
I think I am going bright red,
How could he do this, he is being a real pain!

Phew at last the bus comes,
But he sits next to me.
Now he's doing a car impression,
So I'm trying to pretend that I can't see!

The bus journey took hours,
At least that's how it seemed!
At last we are home,
The day has been worse than I could have dreamed!

We are playing on his computer,
Now he's doing some daft mimes.
We are having a real laugh,
OK so I admit it, he's alright sometimes!

Charlotte Barlow (14)
King Edward VI School

MOVIE PREMIERE!

I've got my pen and paper,
I'm ready to see the stars,
I'm pulling up right now,
Look at all the cars.

There's a big crowd of people,
With cameras, what a flash,
I'm getting out the car now,
I've got to make a dash.

I've just spotted Nicole Kidman,
Her hair's so long and red,
With Tom Cruise on her arm,
I'll write down everything she's said.

She told me about her new movie,
Which she's working on with Brad Pitt,
But to get this part she had to work out,
And get really fit.

I sat down for the movie,
Right behind Tony Blair,
That was such a surprise,
I didn't know he was there.

Once the movie ended,
Everyone headed for the door,
I'd best run now,
And find out a little more.

I had a good night,
But I need to clear my head,
I think I'll go home now,
And get right into bed.

Zoe Porter (13)
King Edward VI School

ODE TO A A MILNE

I write this poem to A A Milne
For his dedication
For the times that I have read his books
Shows my appreciation.
For, walking down the shopping aisle,
I see a piglet on a tin
And looking at the trolley
I quickly pop it in.
What genius composition
It's really rather funny
The times that are spent thinking of Pooh Bear
And his honey.
Conjuring up ideas,
He makes it seem quite easy,
Like when Piglet blew away
On the day when it was breezy.
But ideas kept a rolling
And joined me in my dream
Of Roo playing Pooh sticks
And Eeyore floating down the stream.
So, thank you Mr Milne
For being so very clever,
And when I put pen to paper
I follow my endeavour
To create such a character
And such a story line -
And even if you struggled
In the end it turned out fine!

Jennie McCreight (13)
King Edward VI School

STARTING COMPREHENSIVE SCHOOL

Finished primary,
Feeling cool,
More than ready for comprehensive school.

Six weeks later,
What a shock!
Someone show me to the language block.

Books to carry,
Rooms to find,
All this homework, what a bind!

Hockey practice,
Netball too,
Late for dinner, join the queue.

Different lessons,
In different places,
Search for friends among strangers' faces.

Only 12 more months,
Until we're Year 8,
Then no longer Year 10 bait.

Two weeks later,
Give a shout,
What was all the worry about.

Marie Mckenna (12)
King Edward VI School

SUNFLOWERS

The ever popular sunflower was once
growing in my back garden.

It all started with one little seedling
in a small terracotta pot.

The seedling started to germinate and
grow, it got taller and taller.

I replanted my sunflower into a bigger pot
and let it grow until ready to go into the
outside world.

My sunflower never stopped growing
it grew and grew until it was 15 feet tall.

Then one day yellow petals came out
of the sunflower, it looked just like the sun.

All the petals on my sunflower died,
then the stalk snapped and fell to the floor.

I was sad when my sunflower broke,
but my sunflower was the best by miles.

Jessica Norman (13)
King Edward VI School

SEA MAMMAL!

Born on the water
The finned mammal of the sea
The playful dolphin.

Ben Agar (13)
King Edward VI School

THE BIG DATE

I'm going to meet my boyfriend,
we're going to the fair.
But I'm having a bit of a crisis,
I don't have anything to wear.
I'm wearing blue eyeshadow,
I should wear my short blue skirt,
but then I'll have to wear my crop top
and I'll look like I'm a flirt.
Should I wear my hair down,
or piled up on my head?
If things carry on like this,
I'll say I'm sick in bed.
My red lipstick's melting
and my brown doesn't match my shoes!
A dress, a suit, a skirt and top,
I don't know what to choose.
I've finally decided on my purple dress,
my hair is pinned up nicely
and my makeup looks the best.
My mum says I look lovely
but that I already know,
I'll sit and watch the tele now,
it's three hours 'til I go!

Hannah Osborn (14)
King Edward VI School

THE ALBATROSS

The lord of the skies,
Flapping its wonderful wings,
The graceful sea bird.

Adam Marshall (14)
King Edward VI School

GOING ON THE TRAIL

Going on the trail always falling off.
My dad's hopeless.
With scars on my legs, cuts on my knees
when my dad beats me it's a fluke.
My bike's broken, Dad's is fine
        It's hopeless!

Going through the forest
beating my dad.
Dad flies past
I lose again
Sitting with the Magnum
Dad keeps boasting
        Best out of three!

Paul Johnson (11)
King Edward VI School

THE MANNEQUIN

I'd like to be a mannequin in a top New York store.
To see the yellow taxis whizzing by,
And the tall skyscrapers in the sky.

I would wear a nice long winter coat,
Where all the people passing by would come to gloat.

They would see the price tag bold and broad,
And ask themselves, 'Can I afford?'

My coat has been sold.
At the end of the day, I'm tired of standing
'Hip hip hooray.'

Beth Longden (12)
King Edward VI School

CLOUSEAU THE CAT

Clouseau purrs standing at his dish
Looks to the kitchen for his plate of fish.

Scratch scratch scratch on the door
Here comes Clouseau wanting more.

Clouseau strolls to the airing cupboard door
Stretched out on the very warm floor.

Open the door to the afternoon sun
Clouseau jumps out to have some fun.

Oh what sunshine on this lovely day
Clouseau is out to pounce on his prey.

Russell Swannack (11)
King Edward VI School

DOG

Wherever the dog goes she leaves a mess behind,
She's black and white with floppy ears and really very kind.
She got into the man next door's and ate the squawking hens,
He said that he would shoot her if he saw her there again.
She emptied out the bin one day whilst I was out at school,
She ate the rubbish then was sick and that's not very cool.
She lays underneath the table and makes some awful smells,
Then in a couple of minutes I start to feel unwell.
Dad shouts 'Out you stinking dog get out into your bed.
And if you do another one I'll hit you on the head!'
But when she is not smelly she is really very sweet,
I like her the best at night-time when she's laid down at my feet.

Tom Heath (11)
King Edward VI School

FRIENDS

Friends forever
Our friendship's everywhere.

I thought we would be
Friends till the very end
Whatever happened to my friend
What happened on that night
Did we argue,
Did we fight?

Friends forever
Our friendship's everywhere.

All I want is to say I'm sorry
For all the things I did to make you worry
You're my friend that's what you'll always be
We're meant to be together can't you see?

Friends forever
Our friendship's everywhere.

Kerriann Flynn (12)
King Edward VI School

ENGLAND!

Beckham has skill,
As much as a will.
Seaman gets rich,
By playing on the pitch.

Shearer tries to score,
His shot was very poor.
Owen has a run,
He found it really fun.

Ince takes a kick,
He felt really sick.
Adams tries to clear,
The attacker has no fear.

Batty turns sad,
The ref gets mad.
The team played well
Then Hoddle fell.

Michael Stock (12)
King Edward VI School

F1 RACING

Maclaren team are the best,
This year Schumacher's been a mess,
The Jordan are doing OK,
Hakkien is the best,
Better than all the rest,
With 95 points he is surely the best,
Schumacher is close behind,
Faster and faster all the time,
In the chicane weaving in and out,
Taking over on the corners,
Spinning off the cars are out of order.
Five more laps then the chequered flag.
Schumacher is coming up fast
I think he is going to crash
Coming up to the last bend,
Getting closer to the end,
Here they come around the last bend,
Schumacher crashes right near the line,
Hakkien wins from Schumacher's mistake.

Scott Bartle (11)
King Edward VI School

DRAGONS

Dragons, dragons
Breathing fire and smoke,
Sleeping in the highest mountain caves,
Taking deer and cattle from wood and field
Burning down villages and woods.
Feared by so many
But some so tame
They wouldn't hurt a fly
Apart from by mistake.
But some kill, murder
And terrorise anything
They have great mounds
Of gold and silver.
They guard these treasures day and night
There's even a river of molten gold
Where a dragon spat a fireball
Or a man tried to enter and it
Breathed fire at him.
Many men have tried
To kill this mighty beast
But have failed and perished
More men have died than have succeeded
In killing the mighty *dragon.*

Rowan Holliland (11)
King Edward VI School

My Rabbit

I have a rabbit called Bisto,
And he is a fussy rabbit,
He hides his food in the morning
So I have to stroke him
Then he will get it for me.
When he wants a saltlick
He will eat the cage door.
Bisto is a smart rabbit
Because sometimes he hides his treats
Under the food
But he throws half of the food around
To get the treats.
When I put his food bowl in the wrong place
He will move it with his nose to the right position.
When he has to go to the vet we have to pick him up
Which he doesn't like
So we hide the pet box so he doesn't see it
But he can sense it
So he hides in his bed,
Bisto's got a run at home
And when he hasn't been in it for a long time
He tries to pull the wire off and get out.
My grandad has got a dog and when it comes
They sniff each other's noses.
Bisto is a very funny rabbit
Because he jumps around like Jumping Jack.

Jason Todd (11)
King Edward VI School

A CAT CALLED ARTIE

I have a cat called Artie
He is an old cat is Artie
In our years he's 17
In his years he's 119
But still we love him dearly.

He's a friendly cat is Artie
He's a big tabby cat is Artie
He's furry and cuddly
His miaow is funny not like a cat's
But still we love him dearly.

When I was young I pulled him about
And he always dodged me when I was around
But now I'm older he's a lot bolder
He even sits on my knee and purrs
I really love him dearly.

He's a big tabby is Artie
He's been in quite a few fights
But he always comes back OK
So now you know my cat called Artie
And really we love him dearly.

Matthew Duke (11)
King Edward VI School

TESS'S NEW START

Unwanted in a line of pens,
Waiting for that someone.
Someone who could give me love
Who I could trust
Who would care for me and play.
But people passed me by
Did anyone want my love?
But after all that time I'd just given up.
The next day I was lucky
A man, woman and their daughter
Pointed at me and said
Isn't she lovely but why is she lying in bed?
Later on that afternoon it was said
I was to live with them
I jumped into the car and thought
Is this the happy ending I've always wished for?
Later on in the night they put me in the kitchen.
I thought I'd been dumped again
But in the morning I knew how silly I'd been
For there they were patting and stroking me
I know I've got a happy life now
But I'll never forget those sad lonely days
When I was in the kennels in the month of May.

Anneka Eggleston (11)
King Edward VI School

STREET HOCKEY

Blades on my feet, stick in my hand,
I play hockey like the best in the land.
Pads on my elbows, pads on my knees,
See me play like Wayne Gretzky.
Wheels rotating round and round,
See them going at the speed of sound.
Slap shot!
Wrist shot!
I practise these an awful lot.
Blading forward with such pace
I would surely win a speed skating race.
When I'm near the net,
I pose an enormous threat
Especially when I raise my stick
Then it will only take a tick
To blast the yellow hockey ball
Into the top of the goal
Before the keeper has a chance to call
Damn it, he's made it one all!

Jonathan Wadsworth (11)
King Edward VI School

AM - PM

Darkness, a black velvet sky
Stars twinkle at night
The moon gives us light
Brightness, heat, the sun's warm glow
Making grass, trees and flowers grow
Night and day.

Nicola Hulls (11)
King Edward VI School

My Dog

I have a dog
my dog called Hog
he is brown and black
like a dirty cat.

He loves running
but also hugging
he is running like the wind
he is sleeping like a king.

He came to England
before two years
he is so cute
like a silver flute.

He will never bite you
if he doesn't like you
'cause he knows you are my friend
he will lick you again.

Stefania Toufexi (12)
King Edward VI School

The Summer Sun

Children play under the hot summer sun
They play all day and can always run.
They play happily in the long grass
Leaving tracks as they pass
They break for a drink
They go swimming but never sink
They play football that's great fun
And summer is over but winter's just begun.

Andrew Scott (11)
King Edward VI School

JOB

My dad says I should be a jockey
but my uncle says I should play hockey.

My mum says I should be a cook
but my aunt says I should write a book.

My brother says I should be a fighter
but my sister says I should be a writer.

My gran says I should work on a liner
but my grandpa says I should be a miner.

My cousin says I should be a zoologist
but I say I should be an archaeologist.

Which one should I choose?

Luke A'Bear (11)
King Edward VI School

BENJI AND CHUCKY

Benji has been with me all my life
We've had good times and bad.
Benji makes me laugh
And stands by me when I'm sad.
Chucky has been here, for one year
But Chucky also makes me laugh
Especially when he has a bath.
I thank God for letting me
Have such pets as Chucky and Benji
At last.

Susan Ingamells (11)
King Edward VI School

THE LIGHT OF MY LIFE HAS GONE AWAY

The light of my life has gone away,
Left before I was able to say,
You were the one I loved the most,
But now your presence is like a ghost.

We were always together, never apart,
You became an important piece of my heart.
You held my hand and made me feel strong,
But now that closeness has sadly gone.

You put a smile upon my face,
Which no one can replace.
My love for you will never disappear,
My only wish is that you were still here.

Now that you're no longer with me,
People are unable to make me see,
That life has to carry on,
Just like our famous love song.

Vicki Perkins (15)
King Edward VI School

AUTUMN

Autumn time is here
Leaves on the trees turn to golden brown
Leaves which fall off with style and grace
Twisting, turning and dancing around
The wind blows them in the air
Then when all is calm and still
They slowly float down to the ground.

Nick Hawkins (12)
King Edward VI School

THE LONELY LIGHTHOUSE MAN

Off, on,
Off, on,
Round and round,
Round and round,
The only warning to be found.

There he sits all alone,
Thinking of his folk back home.

Up and down the steps he walks,
But to no soul does he talk.

The waves crash on the rocks,
Who knows when the storm will stop.

The sea calms down and regains her poise,
But it's often lonelier without the noise.

James Renshaw (14)
King Edward VI School

THE CHURCH WOOD-PIGEON

Every day I go past the church,
I see a very handsome wood-pigeon,
He perches upon the roof of a church gateway.
His feathers are bright, fluffy and beautiful,
His beak is a very pale orange, with funny little nostrils.
I wonder why he perches upon the beautiful roof
Of a church gateway.
It could be a mystery forever,
But one day I will find out.

Sadie Louise Kuzio (11)
King Edward VI School

THE LAST BEAUTY

The gentle breeze runs through the leaves,
Watch them twist and spin and weave.
The gold ripe corn whispers its presence,
Bulging through the old barbed fence.
Songs of birds both high and low,
The evening sun casts its glow.
Long shadows tower over me,
The sky deep blue like a vast sea.
Tufts of green sprout through the path,
Its stony grey contrasts the scene,
The beauty beyond shows it to be mean.
Up on the hill, industry roars,
Swallowing this beauty in its jaws.
Why does man exploit this place?
Its wildness we cannot replace.
Once it's gone it is no more,
Then I shall scream and shout and roar.

Wendy Inman (14)
King Edward VI School

A TIGER

The orange and black tiger
Stalking its prey through the vast savannah
With its soft padded paws
And extremely sharp claws
Hardly making a sound
On the hard dusty ground
Sometimes in luck
And sometimes not.

Laura Kinch (11)
King Edward VI School

WINTER

Trees so bare,
Snow so white,
Ice so cold.
Robins out for winter,
Snowball fights,
Snowmen standing,
Christmas coming,
Nights so cold,
Snow falling down,
Candles glowing,
Foggy mornings,
Shorter days,
Longer evenings,
Fires burning,
Animals hibernating,
Christmas presents.
Winter days,
December, January and February,
Christmas trees up,
Iced over puddles,
Frosted windows.

Linden James Harland (11)
King Edward VI School

DONCASTER BELLES LFC

Saturday is my favourite day,
Out on the field with my team,
Crowds of fans on the sideline,
'Donnie Belles' they scream.

Lining up for that starting whistle,
Butterflies I feel,
The ball's left its starting spot,
This game is now for real.

Running with determination,
This ball's mine I cry,
Going for every challenge,
Someone's gonna die.

It's times like these I love the most,
I just cannot stop,
I'm going to score that winning goal,
Till I'm injured and drop.

Passing the ball from time to time,
We're gonna score a goal,
Tactics here, skills there,
It's one nil we're on a roll.

Fans delighted with our outcome,
Doncaster Belles the best,
They're gonna win the league,
Cos they're better than the rest.

Tracie Newbury (15)
King Edward VI School

WHERE IS THE PAST?

When the sky is blue,
And the clouds are white,
You can't tell time is flying by,
Where does it go?
Does it just disappear into our memories?
Or onto paper?
Or is it forever replaying our lives?
Changing them to form new dimensions,
Could we ever go back in time?
Would the past go back in time?
Would the past be waiting for us?
Or just an empty void?
Will we ever know,
Where is the past?

Victoria Purnell (14)
King Edward VI School

I SAW AN ALIEN

As I was walking through a field one night
I was dazzled by a big bright light
I looked up and to my surprise
A great big ship flew out of the skies
It landed on the ground below
And the alien came out, he was as white as snow
He came up to me and stuck out his hand
And when I touched it, it felt like sand.
He got back into his spacecraft
I can't tell my friends about this
They'll think I'm daft.

Kerry Ward (14)
King Edward VI School

SPINNING HEART

My head is spinning
I can't take it any more
His face haunts me every night
and day.
The love I felt for him has now
gone.
After the hate he lay,
His deep voice, his shining eyes.
I hate him, I hate him . . .
I love him.
My head is spinning
I can't take it any more,
My heart's about to break.

Olivia Crampton (14)
King Edward VI School

SWIMMING

Swimming fast,
Swimming slow,
However you want to go.
Up, down, round and round,
Swimming all the time.
Butterfly, back, breast and crawl,
Whichever you want to do.
Galas, trophies, come right now,
Just try,
You'll see.
Swimming, swimming . . .
Come with me!

Annika Holliland (14)
King Edward VI School

ENGLAND V THE ARGIES

England v the Argies
World Cup '98
We all sit to watch the match
To learn of England's fate.

Argentina score from a penalty
Then we get one as well
Shearer steps up to take it
It's 1-1! The match begins to gel.

A few more minutes pass
Then Owen shows his skill
The ball hits the back of the net
But I wish it was 10-0.

It's now 2-1 to England
And nearly half time
Then the Argies make it 2-2
Set up by their number nine.

The game is into the second half
Then Beckham loses his cool
He kicks an Argie, gets sent off
The fans think he's a fool.

England are down to ten men
And we're nearing extra time
The ref then blows his whistle
The crowd's voices begin to mime.

No goals were scored in extra time
So time for penalties, oh boy!
Batty and Ince miss their kicks
The Argies win, and jump up for joy.

James Waite (14)
King Edward VI School

ME

The sky
Surrounds
Commands
Lines the world
And at sunset
Meets
The ocean
Which reaches
To the ends of the earth
Where it hangs
Before falling
Against the sand
Which makes up
The shore.
The sand
Stretches
'Til it meets the earth
And kisses
And exchanges
And becomes
Brown
Fertile and clean
Covers the land
A thick blanket
Of softness.

It squidges between my toes.

Amy Law (14)
King Edward VI School

BEACHES, COVES AND CAVES

Beaches are amazing places,
With sea, sand and rock pools.
But don't forget the best places of all,
The little coves and hidden caves.

The coves are really quiet,
Only the sound of the waves can be heard.
Inside the caves there are different sounds,
Your footsteps echoing, and water dripping from the walls.

The cobbles under your feet,
Are slippery, wet and covered in green slime.
As you leave the outside world behind,
The excitement starts to build up inside.

The exciting thing is you never quite know,
What you might find around the next corner.
Part of a shipwreck, some nice driftwood,
Or maybe just a dirty old boot!

Ella Pearson (14)
King Edward VI School

MY FAVOURITE POSSESSION

A most favourite possession is
a teddy bear from my mum and dad.
It's pink and purple, yellow and blue
and best of all it says 'I love you.'
It is up in the attic just like new
my sweet little teddy
I love you.

Sarah Taylor (11)
King Edward VI School

PARENTS

Parents,
You either love them or you hate them.
Either way they're always there,
Telling you to clean your room,
And sealing in your doom.
Always saying don't pick on your sister,
Or never pick a bulging blister.
Saying never pick at your food,
And will you stop being so crude.
Always telling you not to be home late,
And have you shut the garden gate.
So this poem concludes,
That no matter what you do,
Parents are always there for you.

Emma Foulds (14)
King Edward VI School

SECRETS

Secrets can be mysterious, deep, dark and black,
They come in different sizes, but there's one thing they lack.
The chances to be open, bright, bold and sharing,
Tell them only to friends who are trusting and caring.
There's small ones, big ones and the ones in between,
Secrets hide around corners never to be seen.
Secrets are things not everyone can know,
So don't shout it out or take it that low.
Keep your secrets, remember what they're about,
And make sure of this one thing, they *never* get out!

Rebecca Barton (14)
King Edward VI School

SOAP STARS

I love to watch my favourite soaps,
Night after night they give me hopes,
That my dull life might never be,
As fraught as theirs is on TV.

Their worlds unfold night after night,
I live their lives with great delight.
Safe and sound in my own room,
Far away from all their gloom.

It can't be true, it can't be real,
Living life like Cindy Beale.
I think I'll stop before it's over,
I might end up like Cathy Glover.

Judith Iles (14)
King Edward VI School

TEENAGE TURMOIL

The world is turning,
But I'm standing still.
There's night and day,
But I only see darkness.
There's four seasons,
But I feel only winter.
There will always be downs,
But I look forward to the ups.
I'm always turning from left to right,
I guess,
I'm on the never-ending roller-coaster
Of teenage life.

Elaine Chambers (14)
King Edward VI School

RIP Doncaster Rovers
75 Years In The Football League

The Rovers fans turned up at Chester
only three points will do and Hull to lose.
When the ref blew the ground smelt like a public loo
on seven minutes Chester scored
Doncaster Rovers were going out the door.
Then on 17th that man A Mike bagged the goal
that they needed to stay.
Then on 43 the man with the first name of P
scored for Chester.
The fans were screaming at Doncaster
when the ref blew the final whistle the fans
were crying like hell around the ground.
The songs were sung, we'll support you for evermore
'You'll never walk alone'.

Dan Wynn (13)
King Edward VI School

Footy

Football, football, football, what's it all about
The players come on the pitch and the crowd begin to shout.
They run around the pitch tackling for the ball,
A player gets injured and he begins to fall.
The ref goes into his pocket, he looks a little cross,
He shows the red card and tells them who's boss.
Player shoots then scores
One more goal and it's not a draw!

Now you now what it's all about
Get up and find out.

Daniel Anderson (11)
King Edward VI School

SHINING LIGHT

I am setting off on my journey,
My journey through life,
Along the long and winding road,
That I must travel.
I am guided by that shining light,
Which shows me where to turn.
Its radiance cheers me,
And gives me strength to fight the shadows.
I peer into the light,
Within its flames I can see,
A beautiful girl smiling back at me.
Her silky, golden hair illuminated by the flame.
I reach out to touch her,
But she jumps back.
So I carry on with my journey.
When I need to sleep,
I curl up with my light beside me,
Keeping watch over me, protecting me.
When I am travelling to my destiny,
I fear no evil because I know,
I will always have beside me,
My beautiful and radiant,
My one and only,
Shining light.

William Law   (14)
King Edward VI School

FAMILY

My family at dawn
I wish I'd not been born
Stomping, shouting, mardy kids
I wish I was the only kid
My brother moaning
My mum is groaning
I wish I lived alone
I would never moan
No mess around
And no loud sound.
From my bedroom
Came the sound of clattering bangs
And shouts and cries
It's 8.30 I'm not surprised
'It's time for school'
'Not a game of pool'
'Get dressed'
'Where's my vest?'
'Get my lunch
Get the best bunch'
'Goodbye'
The house is empty
My mum lets out a sigh
Six and a half hours till the chaos returns.

Amy Depledge (11)
King Edward VI School

MY BOOK

Here in my book is a fountain,
a river, a forest and a mountain,
a genie, a princess, a goat,
an ogre and a castle with a moat.
I'm looking in my book for adventure
but where to find it I can't be sure
and when I'm at this adventure's end
I'm sure I'll go looking for more.

In my book there's a pirate and a
treasure chest
and a buzzing bee being a pest.
A rat, a mouse and a creepy old house
a cuckoo, a kangaroo and a monkey
in a zoo,
a cat, a rat and a magical mat.
That's what's in my magical, marvellous,
wonderfully made book!

Laura Suchorzewski (11)
King Edward VI School

FUNNY FOOD

Steak and kidney pie makes me want to cry,
I want a tasty treat, something I like to eat.
Fruit and veg, Mum's gone in the head.
A little bit of soup makes me want to puke,
But something tasty will be made of pastry.
Chocolate ice-cream would be a dream.
Overall, chips and beans rule supreme.

Simon Adams (13)
King Edward VI School

THE FAIR

The fair is a wonderful place,
It comes twice a year.
It doesn't come very often,
But when it does we cheer.

There are so many rides to choose from,
You just can't make up your mind.
But you have to queue up quickly,
Or you'll get left behind.

The fair will come back soon,
Probably in early November.
I hope the fair comes back soon,
When it does I'll have to remember.

David Highfield (13)
King Edward VI School

FISHING

Fishing is very relaxing and calming
it's something I can do with my dad
whether it rains or shines
it won't change my mind
fish or not fish I won't be mad.

Every Sunday morning
I get up bright and early
I put together my tackle and bait
and off to the lake I go
I'd go fishing every day if I could
because I enjoy it so much.

Greg Jones (11)
King Edward VI School

LIFE'S LIKE A BOX OF CHOCOLATES

Yesterday was sunny
Like the Strawberry Surprise
Last week I was angry
Like the Bitter Coffee Treat
Saturday was raining
Like the Orange Cream
Washing into my mouth
Today I was glowing
Like the golden wrapper of the
Hazelnut Swirl
But tomorrow you tell me?
Because you never know what you're
Going to get!

Claire Edson (14)
King Edward VI School

DREAMERS

I am sitting on a train and in walks a zebra in a waistcoat,
serving tropical punch.
He says 'Look out of the window'
I do and I see seated upon a star, a dragon reading a newspaper.
I turn to the zebra and say 'Where are we going on such a blissful day'
'Night' he corrects me, 'to some imagination'
He passes me some X-ray specs and says 'Come this way'
We walk to the luggage and I put on the specs
I look at the luggage and I see a double bass but hiding inside
are three crocodiles.
I say 'To whose imagination are we travelling'
and with a gleam in his eye he says . . .

Becky Wine (13)
King Edward VI School

LOVE

Like ripples on water,
Like falling leaves in autumn,
Like lambs in spring,
Or the sun in the sky,
It's part of nature.

No set age
Not in my eyes,
Girls, boys, men and women,
People fall into it so easily
But it's so hard to get out.
Feelings unravel like a
Knitted jumper.
No matter how hard
It all has to come out . . .
Sometime.
Love.

Annie Bethell (15)
King Edward VI School

STILL WORKING

My name is T20 Ferguson
Fergie for short
I am a small grey tractor
I am useful for all sorts
Even though I am very old
I am as reliable as a trusty cart horse
In all weathers I never fail to start
From ploughing, sawing or pulling the farmer's cart.
So next time you're in the country out
There's sure to be a T20 somewhere about!

Christopher Marsh (13)
King Edward VI School

RUGBY

Both teams bind together,
the mis-shaped ball, made up of leather,
gets thrown into the anxious scrum,
teams tighten their grip, the battle commences,
with all our strength we push like mad,
as the ball is released.

Down the wing the ball goes,
nearer and nearer to the try line,
the ball is there,
but tragedy, the fullback tackles him,
with one mighty blow,
the crowd goes *wild*,
with the try yet to be scored.

Anil Jootna (13)
King Edward VI School

WINTER

The dew on the early morning grass,
Winter's here, autumn's passed.
The snow falls gently to the ground,
The feeling of Christmas is all around.
The frost on the window panes,
And the ice on the country lanes.
That summer tan begins to fade,
And you're wearing jumpers that your gran made.
Scarfs, hats and woolly gloves,
It's the time that everyone loves!
At last, winter's here,
It's my favourite time of year.

Sharon Walker (15)
King Edward VI School

DO THEY REALLY KNOW?

They say that you can't fall in love at fourteen
But what do they know!
Do they see things through your eyes?
Do they feel the pains inside?
Do they feel the beating of your heart?
Do they feel the hurt when you're apart?

Do they see the twinkle in his eyes?
Do they see your loving ties?
Do they feel the things you feel?
Do they know your love is real?

They think you like their advice
They think you think they're being nice
But you can keep your feelings inside
As long as he stands by your side.

Claire Hancock (14)
King Edward VI School

MY NEW BIKE

My new bike is top of the range
That's quite funny cos it's an orange
No it's not a drink and it's not a fruit
But to go real fast it needs some good boot
Sometimes in the morning I do ride dead fast
And on some of those times I get to re-taste my breakfast
I don't know why I keep on doing it
I really really really hate it
In fact whilst writing this poem
I feel I've found sense
And next time I *will* make amends.

Sam Chambers (14)
King Edward VI School

THE NIGHT SKY

The never-ending flow of people
In and out of pubs and clubs.
You sit and look up at the stars,
Wondering who or what they are.
The black of night closes in around you,
With only the moon as your guiding light.
The animals that live for the dark,
Make strange noises in your heart.
Your eyes closing, darkness sets in.
Sleep overcomes your body.
Tired and cold,
Knowing that soon the sun will come up.
The light of day, to soon show its face,
But the dark still surrounds you,
Looking up at the night sky
The planets, the brightest in the sky,
Shine on you, a big bright star.
As you walk back to the light and warm
The night is left behind and the day draws near,
Warm and light fills your heart.

Alexa Marsh (14)
King Edward VI School

CHOCOLATE

Delicious, gorgeous and creamy,
Delightful, dark and dreamy.
It comes in dark, milk and white,
What a lovely thing to bite.
My stomach always rumbles,
When that chocolate crumbles.

Rebecca Walker (11)
King Edward VI School

GUESS WHO

Handsome and charming, that's what he thinks
I wonder how many grey hairs we've lost count.
Stopped counting, and what about the laughter lines,
What size waist?
For every ounce there is a smile, a joke,
Even if he does laugh at his own.
He laughs, we all laugh at him, with him,
Even about him.

Annoying? Oh yes he can be.
Impatient? Almost all the time,
Flicking through the Teletext,
Watching news after news after news.

There's always a smile for Liverpool
But it's not always the case when they lose,
But then it's the ref's fault.

Table tennis is the sport,
He always thought he was rather good.
I suppose he is really but we don't let him know that.

He's alright my dad.

Sarah Hughes (13)
King Edward VI School

THE SEA

The sea is a starving ferocious wolf
Stalking for its prey
Inch by inch by inch it creeps up to the shore
With its sharpest claws
Trying to get ready to pounce on a helpless crab.

Leighann Bell (11)
King Edward VI School

BOYS AND GIRLS

B oys
O pen to the air
Y oung love
S exy

A dolescents
N aughty
D irty

G irls
I gnorant
R ich in talk
L oyal and loving
S ad.

Stephanie Harrison (12)
King Edward VI School

MY FRIEND

I have a cute friend, I know she isn't real
She has long blonde hair
With tiny feet
She's rather small
I see her most nights, in my dreams
She's lonely unlike me.
She has no family
Not many friends
Only me, she knows,
Who thinks about her, the way she grows
I know she's not much
But she's a friend
An imaginary friend to me.

Lacey Redford (11)
King Edward VI School

STOP THE NOISE, CUT OUT THE POWER

Stop the noise, cut out the power
Let the heavens send us an almighty shower.
No more autumn, winter, summer, spring
Let the lovers have their final fling.

No more travel, just stay put
There's no more use for the job of the foot.
Hide away for the rest of my days
Lock up the child that happily plays.

Tell the hot sun it can't rise anymore
It must sink away to the earth's middle core.
Close all the doors and put down the latch
Take laughter and voices and blow out the match.

From the second you took your last breath of air
Everything ended, I just didn't care.
My world has closed with everything in it
And I wish to God it had taken me with it.

Rebecca Osborn (15)
King Edward VI School

THE BEACH

I pick up a handful of golden sand
And let the grains slip through my fingers.
A seagull swoops the sky above
And lands down on the ground.
The seagull picks at the leftovers
While I look at the sky and wonder why
The beach is so beautiful.

Rosie Edson (11)
King Edward VI School

Turn Off The Music, Turn The Light Out

Turn off the music, turn the light out,
All my dreams just bring me doubt.
Silence of the clock,
Who needs the tick tock?

Don't let the gate go, no knocking at the door,
There is no need for night or day anymore.
No more need for a clear blue sky,
My lover has left me, please tell me why?

My clothes look dull, nothing looks right,
I know my heart doesn't need a fight.
I have to let go my universe is gone,
I wish he hadn't left me, he's the one.

Michelle Hancock (15)
King Edward VI School

Spiders

Spiders are ugly,
With their eight hairy legs,
And two beady eyes,
Which stare at your head.

They're all different sizes,
Large and small.
Some have large bodies,
Which helps them to crawl.

So this poem concludes,
That all spiders are cruel,
They go around scaring people,
When we're at school.

Claire Foulds (12)
King Edward VI School

A BIRTHDAY TREAT

I'm going shopping today
to buy a new dress
it's for my birthday
a present from aunt Bess.

She sent me the money
with my birthday card
it's only five pounds so
I'll have to look hard.

My mum says we should go
to Oxfam or Netto
I suggest Armani
she says 'You must be barmy.'

We went into town
and had a look round
and then I found
I'd lost my five pounds!

Jennifer Longden (11)
King Edward VI School

DOLPHINS UNDER THE SEA!

Dolphins dolphins under the sea
Can you hear them call to me?
They glide so gracefully under the deep blue sea
Up they jump in and out, all around.
Do you hear them call to me upon the ocean top?
Their skin so smooth they are so fast
Diving around in the deep blue sea.
If you are quiet you might hear them call to me
Upon the ocean top.

Lisa Kirk (11)
King Edward VI School

CROOKED TOOTH

The waves crashed on the shore
As a dark man stole away
His face was black
His cloak was black
When he opened his mouth
One tooth stuck out in the centre
Then just like he had come, he disappeared

A dagger was dropped
It bore the symbol of his teeth
It was also freshly stained with blood
Far away a man lay dead
In a pool of blood, and bore the same mark
The mark of the *crooked tooth.*

Peter Sowerbutts (11)
King Edward VI School

TIME TO GO

What told the swallow
It was nearly time to go
Although the crops were golden
Something told him 'Snow'
Leaves were green and rustling
Berries were rosy and glossed
Even though he's happy
Something told him 'Frost'
I wonder what told the swallow
It was time to fly
Summer warmth was ahead
Winter left behind.

Sarah Garnett (13)
King Edward VI School

LONELINESS

I feel alone,
In the dark,
I can't control it,
It's in my blood, in my heart.

I don't know what it's all about,
It's just depression,
Everyone gets it no doubt.

You'll probably be in a muddle,
But definitely no trouble,
The bully is found,
You are free,
Don't let it go too far, not out of bounds.

Now you'll feel fine,
You'll soon see the friendly sign,
And I'll be here waiting for you!

Megan Levi Bird (13)
King Edward VI School

FRIENDS

Friends are meant to stick together,
Friends are meant to stay that way
Forever.
From young to old,
Their friendship holds together.
Friends are friends whatever,
Friends can weather all weathers
And friendship ends,
Never!

Sarah Pryor (12)
King Edward VI School

THE SPOTTED SPHINX

The spotted sphinx, the Masai Mara champ
can win in just one way,
With his sudden bursts of awesome speed
he will outrun his prey

A cunning trip at breakneck speed
is all that it will take
To send a little antelope
tumbling in his wake

His large brown eyes
his silky fur,
His lanky mottled limbs
it's only when he eats well that he begins to purr

And so the king of flat out speed
settles down to rest,
He thinks about what he's to eat
and choose which is best

Who is the prince of all the plains?
You may or may not know,
He is if course the cheetah
who over the plains will flow.

Thomas Elliott (11)
King Edward VI School

FOOTBALL

You can watch it or listen with your ears,
See the blood, sweat and tears.
Twenty two players and a ball,
Beckham's up make a wall!

The whistle is blown, battle commences,
Each team has tight defences,
If you lose burst into tears,
Go to the bar and have a few beers.

Mark J Carnall (11)
King Edward VI School

MY DAMN DOG

I have a dog that's black and white
Until she rolls in the mud
Then she's brown, not black and white.

I have a dog that always barks
Even when I walk through the gate
When she goes outside she will dig a hole
Until she finds a stick or a bone.

I have a dog who always moans
When she even has a bone
When we're playing ball and bat
My dad tells her that she should be sat

I have a dog that chases cats
Until the cats are chasing rats
When we are playing with a ball
She will always stand tall

I have a dog that is always hungry
Even after she has had something yummy

I have a dog which is usually naughty
But I know that she is really sweet.

Benjamin Matthews (11)
King Edward VI School

FOREST

In the forest walking slow
Turn around
Sssh
Be quiet
Don't make a sound
Quick, run . . .
I can hear them coming
Run, run as fast you can
Out of the forest
To another land.

Can you hear the rustling sound
Of the leaves down on the ground
You can hear the buzzing bee
And the crashing, whirly sea.

But . . .
They're still coming
Don't wait to see
Just run, run, run . . .

Hayley M Boswell (12)
King Edward VI School

MY PET

My pet is a bit unusual he is a leopard gecko,
He eats crickets,
He walks around his tank in a funny way
He stalks the crickets and then pounces on them
He has a big piece of bark in his tank
That he hides under all the time.

Daniel Murphy (11)
King Edward VI School

THE FLY ON THE WALL

I am a fly on the wall,
Listening to what people say,
Watching their every movement,
Day after day after day.

Sometimes you want to be me,
See what I get to do,
But when I see a swatter,
You don't know what I go through!

I sometimes meet famous people,
The other day I met the queen,
I'd love to see a whole pop group,
But my number one is Mr Bean.

People really do hate me,
They think I am a pest,
But no, I am not really,
I'm just tiny compared to the rest!

When I go to bed at night,
I sleep on your bed,
Mostly I sleep on the middle,
But I sometimes sleep on your head.

I wake up very early,
Just like an early bird,
I creep around very carefully,
But I know that I won't be heard!

I am a lonely fly,
I haven't got one friend,
But I have got a habit,
Of driving them round the bend!

Kerry Brewer (13)
King Edward VI School

SILENT PEOPLE

Silent people gather all around,
Tears will soon fall to the ground.
His body lies on a steel plate,
No one was there, goodbyes are too late.
Weeping softly, their eyes flood with tears,
The atmosphere is full of our deepest fears.
Lifeless, still, stiff and cold,
This body no longer has life to hold.
Pain in the heart is a desperate thing,
A glimpse of sadness in the funeral hymns.
Daytime is dark, joyful sounds are nothing but a muffle,
Not even the little mouse can be heard, while he gently scuffles.
Cries through pain can be heard by those that listen,
Keep looking for the tears, while they all glisten.
Weeping willow's tears are lost,
My darling had to pay the final cost.
Who is there now to dream our dreams?
The world is so empty now that it so long ago seemed.
How I longed to feel the sunlight upon my delicate skin,
It was your touch I longed for, now sunlight is my sin.
The sun has no light, the moon has no song,
The joy in this world has for eternity gone.
The birth of a child is such a happy day,
Shut out all the joy, birth is death's dismay.
Nothing is left but darkness and sorrow,
Happiness will only come, if we ever reach tomorrow.
Weeping willow sing your song,
Of my love that has now gone.
My weeping willow's tears still flow,
Never could they hide my woe.
Weeping willow stop your tears,
Life is full of deepest fears.
The world will never be the same,
Always full of my aching pain.

Tears still flow upon this land,
But in this world, my tears are smaller than the sand.
The angels now his soul keep well,
But round your grave still gather silent people.

Victoria Prest (15)
King Edward VI School

RAINFOREST

I opened the door,
The breeze came in,
I could smell it in the air,
The death of Mother Nature,
The burning of her heart,
The cries of the wild,
The killing of the bush.

Just like that,
Gone,
Destroyed,
The rainforest gone.

I open the gate,
The fire was gone,
All that was left was ashes and smoke.
Black, black, black,
Nothing but black,
Years of growth destroyed.

Wasted,
Disappeared,
Dead.

Tom Renshaw (12)
King Edward VI School

YELLOW!

Yellow is hot
Yellow is bright
It's not the kind of colour that
Would give someone a fright!

Yellow is happy
Yellow isn't sad
It's not the kind of colour that
Will make someone mad!

Yellow's for a boy
Yellow's for a girl
It's the kind of colour you'd
Associate with a pearl.

Simon Chambers (12)
King Edward VI School

THE DRAGON

Just a ball of shimmering scales,
Surrounded by golden coats of chain mail.
His claws are made of silvery steel,
To stealthily devour his next meal.
His eyes shine like the morning sun,
And the knights will not fight but cower and run.
His tail is like a harsh lashing whip,
And his tongue is a flickering black flame behind soft curled lips.
His wings are a delicate web of twine,
In the moonlight his teeth glitter and shine.
For he is the dragon so stealthy and cunning,
From him the people go screaming and running!

Gemma Crossland (12)
King Edward VI School

TEACHERS AND SCHOOL

I have loads of teachers
I have loads of subjects too
Like languages, history and science too
Drama, IT and music, that I like to do
PE, HE, and CDT they're all wonderful too
Art, tutor period, they are cool too
Mrs Dodd and Mr Rizzo teach me English and maths
Uniform is unusual, green, red, white and blue
Mme Emanuel Smith teaches languages too
I have loads of friends in my class
They help me too and that's true.

On Wednesday at about one o'clock
I sing in the choir with some friends
After that back to lessons, CDT I think
We finish at 3.25 I run home so quick
My mum made a brilliant pick
Of this school, this school is super slick.

Vanessa Dobson (11)
King Edward VI School

WALKERS CRISPS

As you take that irresistible bite,
into the Walkers Crisps packet so tight.
The flavour bursts inside your mouth,
They make a fantastic crunch, from north to south.

Ready salted, prawn cocktail and chicken too,
made with the best potato chips just for you.
When they have gone you shriek 'Want more,'
The unique taste has left your heart so sore.

Robert Freeman (13)
King Edward VI School

THE DRAGON SLAYER

A mysterious man was stood beside a gloomy cave, waiting.
A sudden roar broke the silence,
and out of it came the enormous fire breathing dragon!
The mysterious man lifted his sword and it glistened in the moonlight
it roared down then,
amidst the gloomy darkness a dragon was laid across the dusty ground.
The man stood up with triumph.
He did not know what curse was over this ferocious dragon.
It turned to its original figure.
Who was it he wondered, he turned her over.
He had killed his own wife.
He fell to his knees in sorrow . . .
A mysterious man, the dragon slayer, knelt beside a gloomy cave,
crying.

Rhys Bethell (12)
King Edward VI School

SUMMER

Leaves so green,
People playing football,
Surfing on the sea,
Sun so hot.
Birds feeding on feed,
People on holiday,
Fish swimming in the sea,
Drinks all over the place,
Food in shops,
People swimming in the sea.

Ian Dickson (12)
King Edward VI School

WHY?

She sheepishly limps
Into the cold, dark eerie cell
She'd only just grown up
Yes, they had bullied her
But was that a good reason to kill?
No one would have thought she could stoop so low
She had her whole adult life to live
In a free world
But now she would spend it rotting
Decaying
In a high walled, barbed wired
High security
Dismal prison
Did she really resent them that much?
Why did she do it?
Why couldn't she stop herself?
Her life wasn't worth living now
Why?

Gemma Jones (12)
King Edward VI School

GARY THE PIG

There is a pig who wears a wig,
His name is Gary and he will not marry.
When he eats a pie he will fly,
When it's hot he eats a lot.
He runs around when he's happy,
He sits around in mud when he's sad.
He goes bright red and shouts a lot
When he's mad.

Ryan Willows (13)
King Edward VI School

I'VE GOT THE FLU!

I've got the flu
it's absolutely terrible

I went to the nurse
all she said was
'You have just got
a touch of the flu lovey'

I went to the doctor
all he said was
'It will pass over, sorry'

I went to the consultant
he said
'I will give you some
medicine lad'
Yeah! I thought.

Dean Walker (12)
King Edward VI School

ENGLAND FOOTBALL TEAM

Ducking and diving and passing the ball,
Owen strikes it and into the goal.
Then comes Beckham trying to score,
Kicks one of the players who falls to the floor.
The ref has seen him and gets the red card out,
Off you go lad, no messing about.
Now we are struggling with ten men,
But can we do it?
I'm sure we can.

Emma Footitt (12)
King Edward VI School

PINK ELEPHANTS

They play around and make footprints in the ground, they are
Pink
Elephants!
In Pinky Land they are louder than a brass band, they are
Pink
Elephants!
They are really funny and they have no money, but they are
Pink
Elephants!

Running around in circles trumpeting with glee
They are very noisy but don't harm me, they are
Pink
Elephants!

Scott Marshall (12)
King Edward VI School

CRABS

Scuttling here
Scuttling there
Scuttling almost everywhere.

Laying on the ground
Across I scuttle
Nip your nose and start to chuckle.

Up you get
In a rage
Turn around
And complain.

Lucy Walker (12)
King Edward VI School

W,W,WHAT?

W,w,what? Com, gov and dot!
Front page extensions and 'Cumfcave Acbentions',
Hoverbuts, marquees and bots!
FTP or DNS, dot co or was it UK?
How long is this address, will it take all day?

I type in Yahoo! (a search site to you)
It says who, what, when, how, but and why?
I down load a pager, I click on a link . . .
The comp crashed so quickly, I hadn't time to blink!

It booted and beeped and sang a small tune,
I said 'Hurry you stupid . . . or else I'll go *boom!*'
I went to my mail and entered my friend,
'What's that address again?'
And then I clicked
'Send!'

Gavin Keogh (13)
King Edward VI School

KALEIDOSCOPE

A kaleidoscope with so many different colours,
Never twice will the same pattern show.
It always brings joy, not stress or woe.
As you twist and turn, the coloured beads turn and tumble.
No animal shapes will it make not wasp or bumble.
The only patterns it will make are shapes and stars.
Circles, triangles, strips and bars.
Turn it around and a pattern you can make,
Turn it again and the pattern will break.

James Homer (13)
King Edward VI School

MY LITTLE GOLDEN HAMSTER

My little golden hamster,
He lives somewhere under my bed.
He has four legs, a body
And one enormous head.

My little golden hamster,
He's the noisiest thing in the house.
You'd think because he's so small,
He'd be quieter than a mouse.

My little golden hamster,
He scuttles everywhere.
He ends up in your dinner,
And even in your hair.

My little golden hamster,
He's cuter than cherry pie.
Don't tell Mum he's missing,
She'd only break down and cry.

My little golden hamster,
It makes me very sad,
To think he could be anywhere,
If you find him I'll be glad.

Rebecca Allen (11)
King Edward VI School

THE SEA

The sea is like a starving ferocious wolf
Stalking for its prey.
Inch by inch it creeps up to the shore
Waiting to pounce on a helpless crab.

Laura Taylor (11)
King Edward VI School

MY CAT GINGER

My cat Ginger is a lazy bones,
As he lays in front of the fire,
He always waits for a bit of fuss,
And he loves his belly rubbing.
Oh does Ginger love his food;
As I'd say he goes on a diet,
He's getting an old fat cat,
He's out and about on those late, dark nights,
Roaming and exploring the streets.
But now I think he knows, *he's* getting old.
Now he's in for his supper,
Breakfast, dinner and all,
He's still in front of the fire,
Curled up in a tight fluffy ball.

Kerri Sian Lilliman (11)
King Edward VI School

LITTLE ANIMALS

There were two little bears,
That ran up and down the stairs,
And cried for their mummy,
All day long.
When she got there
They were bare,
From crying all day long.

There were two little pigs,
That have wigs.
Because they were bald and bare.
When they went out,
Everybody shouts,
So they bought wigs,
And went out.

There were two little dogs,
With spots on their backs,
That always got chased
By a big black cat.
They'd run here,
They'd run there,
But never get anywhere.

Natalie Hudspeth (12)
King Edward VI School

THE TENT

Me and Amy Grogsey are sitting here in pain
The tent's just fallen down and it's just about to rain.
We scrambled out to try and peg the tent down
in the pouring rain,
Then along came Sarah Clampin with the hammer in hand.
She shouted out 'I found it in the wet and soggy sand.'
We pegged down the last one but oh no where's the fly?
We spent the next five minutes jumping up to the sky.
Then at last I gave Sarah a push up and she managed
to get it from the greenhouse.
Then at last we settled down for the night,
'Oh great' the party next door has just started.
'Are you all right girls? The party's just began settle down
and have a good night's sleep.'
'I want to go to the party. Anyone else who doesn't want
to get their beauty sleep?'
'Oh just shut up now I want to go to sleep.'
'Megan, Amy? I need to water the plants!'
'Oh Sarah! Honestly.'

Megan Geach (11)
King Edward VI School

ATHLETICS

Athletics is a good sport
You can run
You can jump
And you can throw.
You should work hard if you want to be the next
Sally Gunnel
Roger Black
Ewan Thomas
Or Steve Backley
Some people do different events like
Javelin
Discus
Hammer.

Christopher Hart (11)
King Edward VI School

SPACE

I look into the sky,
The stars are wheeling round,
I wonder why
You can never count them all,
There are so many of them,
I wonder why?

Comets flashing past,
Stars shining bright,
Cruising through space,
A beautiful planet is ahead,
A star is behind it,
I wonder where we are?

It is the planet Earth,
We are nearly home,
We smash through the atmosphere,
And down to the ocean below.
We crash into the sparkling blue sea,
The spaceship starts to sink,
The sea rescue come,
I wonder how they knew?

Thomas Spurden (11)
King Edward VI School

MY DOG

My dog is very silly,
As silly as can be.
All she will do every day is sit and wait
For somebody to throw her Frisbee.
She will jump and catch it in her mouth,
And then she will leave it there and stare.
Last year she had nine puppies,
They were as lively as can be.
When they opened their eyes,
They saw where they could bite and nip,
They saw where they could run,
They chased me up and down the garden
And I had to run and run.
My dog got fed up with them,
She used to run and hide,
She used to run up the road,
To her best mate Narla.
They play and scrap and run about,
My dog is very lively like that.

Emily Pilsworth (11)
King Edward VI School

DERIK THE RABBIT

Derik the rabbit is ginger and white,
He never claws with his paws or scratches or bites.
He hops around the garden and loves to roam,
But he never tries to stray from home.
He licks my hands and tickles my feet,
And he loves to flop in front of the fire in the heat.
He loves a cuddle and a stroke on his nose,
But when I have chocolate, believe me he knows!
His nose twitches like mad and I feel very bad
As he jumps onto the sofa and looks very sad.
In the end, I give in and break off a bit,
But before I have even put it down,
He has eaten it!
I put him back in his cage to have a good sleep,
And he hops into his hay which is in a big heap.

Katherine Garton (12)
King Edward VI School

THE HAWK

High flying hawk soaring through the clouds
Scouring the ground for prey.
Shining claws and curled beak ready for a meal
Deep black eyes watching every hole
Long wings waiting, just waiting
For an unlucky victim.

A small brown mouse darts away
Being chased by the hawk
But its little legs aren't fast enough
And it's snatched away from the ground
Away from escape
Away from freedom.

Carried away, far away
Back to the hawk's nest
Shining wings, fast wings
Soaring through the clouds
Shining claws carrying the small animal
Deep black eyes still watching for prey.

Robert Walker (11)
King Edward VI School

CONKERS!

They're chocolatey brown, conkers
You can find them all over town, conkers.

Conkers are seeds
That live in the trees, conkers.

Stick a string through 'em
And you can play games with them
Conkers!

You play in twos
If you get your conker smashed
You lose!

They come in autumn
When the leaves have fallen
Conkers.

You can never be bored with
Conkers.

John Bowmer (12)
King Edward VI School

FAMILY

My brother moans and groans
When he doesn't get his own way
I wish I could go and run away.
He stamps, thuds, shouts, cries and catches flies.

My mum is fun she rubs her tum
Sees some chocolate and shouts here I come.
My mum takes my brother round to Gran's
And Mum tells Gran what a bad lad my brother has been.
Gran says 'Oh what are you like you silly boy.'
So my mum comes home, has a bath and goes to bed.

My dad goes out on Friday nights
Comes back stupid as mice
At the pub he's embarrassing
He jumps on tables, spends £20 and dances on the floor.
So he goes to the chip shop to get some chips
He goes home eats his chips,
Goes to bed and licks his lips.

Kayleigh Skelding (11)
King Edward VI School

WHALES

The whales sail slowly through their soft and silent world
A world that belongs to them
Eating and feeding on a world that might become their grave.

They blow a gush of water
They dive and make a splash
Their singing sounds like harmony
Their tails make a crash.

The whales glide through the deep blue sea
They splash and crash and what do they see
They see us holding nets, playing cards, making bets
As they live under the dark, wavy sea.

They blow a gush of water
They dive and make a splash
Their singing sounds like harmony
Their tails make a crash.

Sasha Summers (11)
King Edward VI School

FRIENDS

Friends are kind
Generous
Loyal
Someone who stays in my mind
Someone who keeps secrets
Someone who sticks up for me
And in a friend I can see -
Someone who is outgoing and loving
My friend and I share hobbies
And always laugh and joke
We help each other with our homework
And swap clothes
When we go out we always have fun
And when we go to each other's house
I know this friend is the one.

Crystal Wilkinson (12)
King Edward VI School

I LIKE FOOD

I like food
When I'm in a mood
For fattening foods
Big plates, small plates
I don't mind
Chips, puddings and pies
Sweets and cakes are my delight
But after all this
I'm no Angel Delight
I'm full and heavy
With a big belly
My head has turned to jelly
So now I'm back in a mood
All because of food.

James Mason (12)
King Edward VI School

SCHOOL DINNERS

School dinners!
The custard tastes like cow muck
The sausages taste like beans
The chips are so well done that
I've only got four teeth!
Everyone used to have them
But no does anymore
They're horrid,
        Disgusting
        Cold and hard
        Absolutely poor!

Craig Swinton (11)
Kirkby Centre School

HOMEWORK

I've got to write a poem
I don't know what about
I've got to think of something
Or the teacher will shout

I have lots of ideas going
Around in my head
Shall I write it now
Or when I lay in bed?

Oh I don't know what to put
Shall I beg, steal or borrow?
Let's forget the whole thing
I'll do it tomorrow!

Johanna Beasley (11)
Kirkby Centre School

UFOs

Big hovering ships, with lights flickering in the sky
UFOs
Like ships of all shapes and sizes, unseen by the human eye
UFOs
People being abducted, by aliens from outer space
UFOs
Extra-terrestrials landing, hoping to conquer the human race
UFOs
Humans being probed, the aliens' methods are really strange
UFOs
I like UFOs, they're mysterious, strange, fascinating and
they're spooky,
UFOs.

Adam Leake (12)
Kirkby Centre School

THE FIREBIRDS

This book is very boring,
This book is very bad,
If I see it one more time
I'll go completely mad.
It will ruin my life forever,
I'll squash it with a car tyre,
I'll cut it into tiny bits,
And chuck it on the fire.
I'll throw it out the window,
I'll throw it out the door,
I'll throw it at the ceiling,
I'll through it through the floor.
I'll throw it in the cupboard,
I'll flush it down the loo,
If I read another book like this,
I'll flush that book down too.
The cover is so horrid,
It's like a baby did it,
If my mother saw it,
She'd have an enormous fit.
It's rubbish altogether,
I'd throw it in the bin,
I'd stick it to a firework,
With a drawing pin.
I'm writing this poem to tell you,
About this book I read,
I'd sooner read a poem book,
Or another book instead.
I'll stuff it under the carpet,
I'll throw it behind the chair,
I'll finish this poem now,
'Cause I don't really care.

Then again I'll do one more,
I'll prove it right now and how,
I'll post it through your letter box,
So you can have it *now!*

Ian Hughes (11)
Kirkby Centre School

TITANIC

The journey of your life
They said -
The safest ride of all
Lay ahead.
Excitement buzzed through this masterpiece,
Passengers waiting for her to sail,
Their only worry - 'Will there be a gale?'
If only this could have been -
But their fate was not foreseen.
In the icy waters - an iceberg lurking,
Which sent this maiden bumping and jerking
Still no one thought they were in any danger.
The ship was unsinkable -
How wrong they could be
Only a few hours before they
Plunged to their death.
Men, women and children -
So many took their last breath,
As the great masterpiece of their time -
Sank
A legend lives on - sadness felt
By many -
That harrowing night
The Titanic lost its way!

Marie Louise Hand (11)
Kirkby Centre School

WHAT IS DEATH?

What is death?
A dark, cold never-ending hole
A ray of light, an endless dream
What is death?
Where do you go?
Where do you end?
What do you see?
No one really knows.

I believe in heaven
Where all goes
A warm, calm, peaceful dream
Mermaids singing, stars twinkling
No wars, no guns, no tears, no anger
Nothing can harm you
Everyone lives in harmony.

I believe in hell
Where all evil goes
A cold, dark hole
Red hot flames sizzling as the sun.
Ice turns to water
Evil turns to ash.

What is death?
No one really knows!

Rebecca Patrick (11)
Kirkby Centre School

THAT'S LIFE

Life is a thing
We all have
Some stay good, some go bad.
We all grow up
With our ups and downs
Sometimes smiles
Sometimes frowns

We can make
Our teachers' lives like hell
When all they want to do
Is teach us to spell

Then the time comes
To go out and get a job
Not just sitting around
Watching telly like a slob

After the story
Of your life's been told
And you get to heaven
(Hopefully old)
When you've had
All the laughs, tears and strife
You can smile and say,
That's life!

Joanne Ward (13)
Kirkby Centre School

When I Was Young

When I was young
I used to play in the heather
But now I'm old
The heather is not there
The motorway lives there

When I was young
I used to play in the stream
But now I'm old
The stream is not there
Toxic waste lives there

When I was young
I used to play in the field
But now I'm old
The dirty old factory lives there

The day will come when I will die
And all my knowledge will pass on by.

Daniel Linfield (12)
Kirkby Centre School

Sports

Sport is a crazy world,
Like tennis and gymnastics too.
If you compete in these events,
You will be crazy too.

Boxing is a mad sport,
Smacking each other on the head.
Boxing is a mad sport,
Until you end up *dead!*

Gareth Hill (11)
Kirkby Centre School

ME

There is a young girl called Amy,
Her parents drive her crazy,
Nagging at this and complaining about that
Saying they've lost things
They're as blind as a bat.
Mum loves yellow and so do I
I love the colour blue, colour of the sky.

I love horses especially 'Socks',
He's only small and could live in a box.
He loves being ridden
Cantering everywhere
Without one single care.

I love football second best,
Michael Owen's the best of the rest.

Catherine is my best friend
She lives not far from me,
She says anything I need she will lend
No matter what it would be.

Amy Peat (13)
Kirkby Centre School

LIMERICK

There was a man from Leeds,
Who swallowed a packet of seeds,
In less than an hour,
His nose was a flower,
And his ears were a bundle of weeds.

Nicky Kiddy (12)
Kirkby Centre School

CHOCOLATE HEAVEN SINCE 1911

Chocolate is nice I eat it, yum, yum
I stuff it down right in my tum
It goes down, gone in a flash
I melt it, drop it, it goes down with a crash
Cadbury's Nestle, I don't mind
You can't have any, aren't I kind?
Lion bars, Mars bars, I'll have them all
As big as a house as big as a hall
I don't leave any, I'm a pig
A chocolate mask, a chocolate wig
Nearly gone, on the last bit
A chocolate tie, a chocolate kit
I have the last bite, it's all gone
I'm not full yet I want a bon-bon!

Wayne Skermer (11)
Kirkby Centre School

ALONE ONCE MORE

Sitting on a comfy sofa,
Drinking a warm cup of tea,
Watching my favourite programme,
I wish you were still here with me.
As I walk slowly up my staircase,
Alone with no one on my arm,
As then I quickly remember,
Your smile and beautiful charm.
The one that had my heart dazzled,
When we first met I was in love,
But now I am so sad and startled,
And you are alone . . . up above.

Nicola Payne (11)
Kirkby Centre School

My Family

My brother's thick,
And as thin as a stick,
My mum's alright,
'Til it gets to night,
My dad thinks he's hard,
But he's as weak as a card.

When my brother eats,
He eats all meats,
And when my mum does too,
She eats her vindaloo,
And when it comes to Dad,
Everyone goes mad.

When we're all asleep,
My brother dreams of sheep,
My mum snores,
Like a wild boar,
And my dad just does it more.

Ryan Greensmith (12)
Kirkby Centre School

My Pet Mouse

First of all my pet's a pain
And my dad said it's always to blame.
Mum said she feels the same
People come in and say what's it's name
It nibbles its paper and makes a mess
My sister said get rid of the pest!

Kelly Bradbury (11)
Kirkby Centre School

MY DOG LADDIE

It was 1993,
When we first met Laddie,
Black and white,
With big brown eyes,
What a gift,
What a surprise!

He protects us every day,
Would-be burglars stay away,
When they hear him bark and roar,
They run away from our door.

We take him for walks every day,
And he has never strayed,
Laddie will be my friend,
Right until the very end.

Adam Hinds (12)
Kirkby Centre School

ALIENS

Aliens live in outer space,
Where no one on earth can go.
Aliens come down to earth,
Every month . . . or so.
Aliens are big-headed,
They know much more than us,
Aliens come down in saucers,
They get exactly what they want.
Aliens live in outer space,
But are they real or not?

David Barnes (12)
Kirkby Centre School

SCHOOL

School is fun,
School is hard to get through,
But it is OK,
Do your best and you will succeed.
School is to learn,
Not to mess,
Get good GCSEs,
Get a good education,
Get a good job,
School is great.

Amy Smith (12)
Kirkby Centre School

BONFIRE NIGHT

Bonfire night is coming soon
The colours in the fire reach the moon
The barbecue flame crackles as the sausages burn
The grown-ups look on with concern.

Matthew Ward (11)
Kirkby Centre School

FRUITY

I like to eat my strawberries and cream
In fact it's almost like a dream
Cherries, berries and raspberries on top
And then I scoff all the lot.

Blake Evans (11)
Kirkby Centre School

RED

Cherries and berries,
Are yummy and scrummy,
Strawberries and raspberries
Delicious desserts,
The watermelon's so bright
It really hurts.
We can't forget
The apples that clean our teeth,
That sat upon
The apple tree leaf.

Crisps inside red crisp packets,
Bright red sweets
That we eat at break.
Then it comes
To school time again,
I dread the thought
Of the teacher's red pen.
She marks my book
Whilst I'm sitting on my red chair,
Thinking
Just look at her red hair.

Roses are red,
Red wine is too,
Love hearts, lips, the sunset sky,
Here I am thinking
Why, why, why?
But I love all these things,
Especially the sky.

Stephanie Reynolds (12)
Kirkby Centre School

MY FAMILY

My name is Stephen
I have a family
They are friendly
They are small

Some are tall
They are young
And they are old

I like to play with my friends
They like football
They use feet playing football
I love my family

Some of my family go to the football match
I go with them
They like to take me
I go to pubs with my family

I play with my mates
I am 13
My birthday is on the 11th of June

My mum and dad called me Stephen
Because they liked the name
Everything is the same
Nothing changes
I like my friends and family
They help me.

Stephen Morgan (13)
Kirkby Centre School

SCHOOL

School, school is so cool,
Food is great, better than my mate,
Teachers are nice,
Only at cost price,
Homework belongs in the bin,
Doing it is such a sin.

I always feel sick,
Because teachers make me sit,
When I get up,
They shout at me and tut.

Then I'm very sad,
And they are glad,
So I want to go home
And sulk.

And that's the poem of school.

Stephanie Scothern (12)
Kirkby Centre School

RED

Red is so nice and hot
It just reminds me of my mum's plant pot
Red, red is so cool
I even think about it sitting on my grandpa's stool
Red, red the colour or red reminds me of grotesque blood
It also reminds me of Little Red Riding Hood.

Lee Turner (12)
Kirkby Centre School

SEVEN AGES OF WOMAN

Stage one is childhood,
so small in the pram.

Stage two, going to school,
in a red checked dress.

Stage three, start adulthood,
getting a new house of your own.

Stage four, giving birth to children,
loving and caring.

Stage five, going on holiday,
showing the children how to camp.

Stage six, now you are a granny,
grey hair and false teeth.

Stage seven, *dead* inside a coffin.

Victoria Cottam (12)
Kirkby Centre School

THE DEVIL

If you've been bad, you won't be glad,
Because hell is the place he is,
It's so hot down there,
He'll give you a scare,
That bad man, *the devil*, doesn't care.

With horns on his head,
He's always painted red,
Be good all your life,
You'll go to heaven when you're dead.

Adam Bramley (11)
Kirkby Centre School

BRAMBLE

My sister's got a rabbit
And it's one year old
It likes to eat carrots
And comes in when it's cold.
He's got long ears
And little feet
He likes to eat milk drops
Because that's his treat.
His name's Bramble
Because he's black
He's soft but wriggly
And doesn't like cats.
I like Bramble
Because he's the best
Out of all the rabbits
He's better than the rest.

Samantha Utting (13)
Kirkby Centre School

BACKSTREET BOYS

Backstreet Boys are the best,
They hardly ever get to rest,
Nick's so gorgeous,
AJ's gormless,
Brian's not bad,
Howie's just mad.

If you haven't heard their music yet,
You had better get cracking
Because the Backstreet Boys
Are just absolutely *smashing*.

Karley Otter (12)
Kirkby Centre School

RED

Red is the colour of the devil's eye
Warm blooded like you and I
It's the colour for rich and royal
Inside of me it makes me boil.

It's the colour of the sunset at night
Reddy yellow so big and bright
While the blazing fire is burning
You're in bed tossing and turning

My cheeks go red as I'm getting angry
My head is about to burst
So I can't write any more
I will put my hand down because
My hands are really sore.

Sarah Scothern (11)
Kirkby Centre School

ABOUT ME

My name is Rob Saunders,
I go to Kirkby Centre School,
I come home at night-time,
And think it's really cool.

Weekend is my favourite time,
I like to drink Pepsi,
It tastes really fine.
I have a PlayStation,
And play on that,
Most of the time.

Robert Saunders (13)
Kirkby Centre School

MYSELF

Matthew is my name,
Football is my game,
I am quite tall,
And brilliant with the ball,
I play at the back,
Never in attack,
I am sports mad,
But that isn't bad.

I like to bath every day,
And use my Lynx spray,
Then when I go to school,
I look really cool,
And ready for the fray.

Matthew Rawding (13)
Kirkby Centre School

ROLLER-BLADING

I enjoy blading
Even when it's raining
I like to get big air,
And this is what I wear
Knee pads, elbow pads
And a helmet over my hair.
I like to go fast,
People watching as I go past
I like to do a sole grind,
You've got to use your mind
I sometimes go slow
When I'm older I want to be a pro.

Paul Cresswell (12)
Kirkby Centre School

MYSELF

My name is Neil,
I have two brothers,
With a good mother,
Who is there all the time.

My dad goes to work all day.
When he comes home,
He likes to play.

I am tall,
With blonde hair,
And blue eyes,
And I like hanging around with the guys.

Neil Whysall (13)
Kirkby Centre School

DESTRUCTION

Destruction, just a word you say,
Yes but what does it represent?
It represents death, panic,
Chaos and pain.
Destruction, whether it be by an earthquake,
Volcano, war, flood or anything else you can think of,
Still represents death.
The panic,
The chaos
And the pain.
It brings tears to your eyes,
And makes you wonder if you're next.
Still think it's just a word?

David Dewberry (13)
Rodney School

MY BABY BROTHER

Every night
Weep, weep, weep
Please, please, please
I can't get to sleep.

Where's my dummy
I feel sick
Get my potty
Quick, quick, quick.

Tickle my tummy
Count my toes
Brush my hair, and
Get my clothes.

Every morning
Wake my mum
Go downstairs
The day's begun.

Hide and seek
Peek a boo
It's my turn
Not him or you.

Here's my dinner
Yum, yum, yum
Feed me please
To fill my tum.

Time for bed
Once again
Weep, weep, weep
I'm in pain.

That's my brother
In the view of my
Mother.

Abigail Gull (11)
Rodney School

IN THE PREP ROOM

Every night at half past six,
I hear a bell 'Bring . . .'
Everyone knows what it's for,
Prep time!
Usually, when everyone has gone in noisily,
You would hear Mrs Finnie shouting,
'Be quiet or else!'
Then there is silence.
But today is different
Instead of sitting down
And marking books,
Mrs Brown is walking around
And taking looks.
She tells people to be quiet,
But doesn't notice much.
She keeps talking and helping
Other people with their prep.
An hour and forty five minutes has gone,
It is time for me to go,
So, I think I'll finish my poem here.

Rainbow Ho (13)
Rodney School

MY LAST REQUEST

I've been hurting for a while now
I tried to be happy, but I've forgotten how.
I didn't know whether I should go on,
I thought I could get over it, it wouldn't take long,
I am sorry for leaving you like this,
But please, I don't want to be missed.
I want to be remembered for the things I hope I did,
I'm sorry if I left you, ran away and hid.
Sometimes I wish I could have lived longer,
But I had to escape, get rid of my anger.
Deep down inside, I need to die,
Now I've done it, I have gone up high,
I'm happy now that I am gone
Happy that I am the only one.
I tried to get it together to keep things straight,
But I failed, now I'm holding the key to the gate.
I couldn't keep up with the pressure of living,
So I died, but hope to still keep giving.
I don't know what your reaction will be,
About me, killing, to leave.
I want everyone to know I am thankful for your help,
But dying is something I've always felt.
I don't want to leave you in pain,
But trust me, we will meet again.
I hope everyone keeps smiling,
For it's my turn now, I'm dying.
I do not feel sad I just feel my time has come,
Goodbye cruel world . . . you have won.

Lynsey Stapleford (14)
Rodney School

SUDDENLY SILENT

The calm clear waters reflect an innocent face,
A child of seven years is staring at himself,
Watching the tears roll off his cheeks and fall
Like drops of lead, shattering the water's surface.

His sister grabs his hand, pulling him through the crowds,
Crowds of people screaming, crying, fighting and looting,
Shops for life-dependant supplies.

Leaving the chaos behind them, they lock themselves
In a tiny back room, cutting themselves off
From the rest of the world.

People outside scream desperate cries; 'Three minutes!
Get inside! The bomb's coming!' Humanity's gone,
Leaving sheer panic in its place.
Two shaking children, two anxious faces,
Waiting for their fate.

Suddenly, there is silence.
Dogs stop howling, babies stop their endless screaming.
A rumble approaches, riding a wave of flames
And a cloud of dust, engulfing everything in its path,
Smothering buildings with its fiery yawn,
Hissing like a herd of volcanic dragons.

The two children lie on the floor, their mouths frozen
In an 'O' of terror.

Nuclear war has snatched away their childhood
Snatched away their lives
Then . . . silence.

Briony Conduit (13)
Rodney School

DANIEL POEM

'You're quiet Daniel' I said
Let's set up the camp bed
We played Star Wars and Playmobil but Tomb Raider scored 10
That was fun let's play it again

KFC was our first meal
We had to fetch it, that was the deal
We watched Lost World on video
All night long but did we though?

We went to sleep late that night
And woke up early with a fright
We went downstairs to play a game
Until we heard Mum and Dad and in they came

We went to Royal Armouries wanting a fight
And out we came with a fright
When we came home it was time for tea
But first of all we needed a wee

Then we watched Flubber
But all it was, was elasticated rubber
Daniel started laughing and so did I
My bursting point is very high

Today we had pains
And had to pack away our games
We made a ship
But it didn't dip.

The bus is late
And this is what we hate
'Now it's the end of that nice weekend' I said
As I scratched my head.

Jordan Miller (11)
Rodney School

SHIPS

Ships are big
Ships are small
Ships are even very tall
Some have guns
Some do not
They are different shapes and sizes.
Some transport people
Some are used for war
Some are used for taking people all around the world.
Some ships are famous
Some ships are not
Some are faster
Some are slower
Some have funnels
Some are just sailing boats with sails.
Some do not have engines
They all have names
Because it is bad luck if you don't have a name.

Daniel Shieber (11)
Rodney School

FOOTBALL

The finest game, the best of all,
But it is more than that.
More than just a game that is played with a goal and a ball.
Football has become a symbol of the world today,
And it is a shame it is not a game of fairness and clean play.

Chris Formon (13)
Rodney School

NUCLEAR WAR

Sirens are sounding,
People are shouting,
Radios announcing,
A warning of two minutes.

The slamming of doors,
Children screaming,
Dogs barking,
The closing of keys in locks.

All of a sudden the loud crash comes,
Bright light flashes,
People blinded,
Babies screaming,
There is quiet,
The radiation has spread.

Katie Shieber (13)
Rodney School

JUDGEMENT DAY

I see it now, judgement day
People screaming, crying
Nuclear war is here,
Then a flash
Person after person,
City after city,
Until the earth is no more.

Jonathan Siddons (13)
Rodney School

FOOTBALL

I like football,
With the round thing you kick.
You hit it with your foot,
You hit it with your knee.
It goes high, it goes low,
It rolls around slow.
It bounces once, it bounces twice,
From side to side it flies.
Bang, bang from foot to foot,
Past the half way line and into the box,
It hits the post!
Back to the foot, back again,
Goal! Roared the crowd.

Kieran Green (11)
Rodney School

NUCLEAR WAR

The bomb has dropped
People are dying,
Places full of dust
Houses destroyed
Blue sky to black
No one and nothing
Heat
Sadness.

Francis Tam (13)
Rodney School

It Had Turned On Me

It's all my fault,
I never should have done it,
I turned around, and I saw it!
I went too far,
I'd passed over,
It had turned,
Turned on me,
I never thought it would be like this,
The pain,
Suffering
And agony.
But clearly, it was the end . . .
Yes the end, of me.

Sophie Frost (13)
Rodney School

Life
(This poem is dedicated to Jared Potter who died on
29th September 1998)

He had a life
He had a dream
He had friends
Until he had nothing
When his life was snatched away
Far too soon.
Now all is left is a memory
A memory of life before death.

Martin Turner (14)
Rodney School

Nuclear Warfare

The nuclear threat everywhere
The towns go quiet
Nothing is to be heard
Suddenly a great gust of heat
Flies across the nation
Destroying everything in its path
People wake to death and destruction
And ask is that the end?
People don't themselves know
People don't care
There's nothing left
It's all over.

Darren Rumfitt (12)
Rodney School

Millennium

Time is running out!
The Year 2000 is approaching,
Computers crashing,
Stock markets flashing,
Fireworks, parties and special events,
A Millennium Dome to represent,
So why all the fuss?
It's only a year and a quarter away,
So if you want to party,
    Get on the bus!

Lance Leivers (14)
Rodney School

TIME

Time passing through and through
the autumn is here
leaves swirling in the air
they fall silently to the ground
a canopy of branches
on the vaulting of the cathedral
the branches splaying.

Time passing through and through
the sky is pink, orange and blue
the sun sets
down, down
until it passes
through and through.

Time passing through and through
rooks' nest swirling, twirling
in the bare trees.
As they land
leaves fall
down, down
onto the silent ground.

Time passing through and through
the leaves falling
rising in the invisible air.

Natalie Shaw (12)
Windmill Ridge Middle School

TIME

Autumn's here
Soft violet sky
Moon rising
Leaves dropping
Swirling, swivelling
Down to the ground.

Under my feet
Trees bare
Waiting to bloom
Under the moon
With the soft violet sky.

The rooks' nests
Lay high up
As the trees' leaves fall
But don't worry spring will come
And it's nearly begun
Under the moonlit sky.

Frankie Bean (11)
Windmill Ridge Middle School

AUTUMN

As the trees sway,
Old leaves fall,
Silently rustling in the wind,
Gazing up at an empty sky.
Rooks swirling and twirling
Down to earth
Waiting for spring
When the birds start to sing.

Joe Forman (11)
Windmill Ridge Middle School

TIME

Time passing
never still
sky violet
feathery moon

Trees fringe the churchyard
almost bare of leaves
branches like the vaulting of the cathedral
splayed against the sky

Rooks diving, swirling
with invisible currents of air
grey ribbed tree trunks
reach up and over

Time passing
never still
sky violet
feathery moon.

Lewis Garrington (11)
Windmill Ridge Middle School

TIME

The night is a curtain,
With holes in the darkness,
The way the light shines through,
Gives the illusion of brightness.

This black velvet curtain,
With its blanket of warmth,
Bathes the world's width,
Until the curtains are drawn.

Ryan Williams (11)
Windmill Ridge Middle School

THE GRAVEYARD AT MIDNIGHT

Time passing,
Leaves falling to the ground,
Watching the wind swirling round,
Trees swaying up and down,
With the darkness of the graveyard.

Time is passing,
Midnight strikes,
Candles flicker,
The clock chimes,
With the darkness of the graveyard.

Time passing,
Stars twinkling,
The moonlight shines,
The inky blackness of the night
With the darkness of the graveyard.

Kelly Emma Cooper (12)
Windmill Ridge Middle School

TIME

Time passing,
Leaves falling,
Dying away,
Wind blowing,
Never still.

Time passing,
Nearly bare trees,
Chestnuts, conkers falling,
Autumn is here.

Thomas Aram (11)
Windmill Ridge Middle School

TIME

The autumn comes
and life's not gone,
the leaves will drop,
but bloom again.

Time will not stop,
through bad times,
go very quick
through good.

Sky shall wander,
but return again
secrets are kept,
not revealed
until,
spring comes round again.

Kate Duffy (11)
Windmill Ridge Middle School

TIME

Grey ribbed trunks,
Over my head,
Hundreds of fallen leaves,
Make a wondrous bed.

Time passing,
Never still,
New leaves, old leaves
Coming through.

Leaves are swirling, twirling high,
Flying round the night blue sky.

Gemma Jankiewicz (11)
Windmill Ridge Middle School

TIME

Time passing,
Leaves falling,
Plants dying,
Waiting for spring.

Time passing,
Conkers, chestnuts tumbling
To the ground.

Time passing,
Bare branches,
Shadowy places,
Birds hovering,
Waiting for spring.

What will tomorrow bring?

Mark Norwood (12)
Windmill Ridge Middle School

TIME

Time is passing as the day draws in
a canopy of branches sways in the wind
bright orange sky with specks of cloud
everything silent.

The swallows circle in the sky
swooping and dancing in the wind
night creatures begin to stir.

The bare trees splay against the church
the last leaf falls from the tree
falling silently
to the earth.

Ashlie Roberts (11)
Windmill Ridge Middle School

TIME

Violent sky
Feathery moon
Time passing
Trees bare of leaves
Branches splayed against the sky
Rooks swirling, rising, falling
Grey ribbed trunks reach up to the sky
Make canopies over the cathedral path
Whilst old leaves fall silent
'Round the young boy's feet and
The ones that lay soft on the path
Go crunch under his feet
Curled and secret leaves wait for
The spring.

Manda Nussey (12)
Windmill Ridge Middle School

TIME

Looking forward
looking back
old leaves dying
new leaves sprouting

Trees almost bare of leaves
delicate branches splayed across the sky
branches towering like a cathedral

Old leaves falling crisp and brown
hundreds and thousands wandering through the invisible wind
feathery moon, violet sky
saying goodbye for the night.

Claire Baggaley (11)
Windmill Ridge Middle School

TIME

Time passing,
Moon rising,
A branched canopy,
Dripping and drooping over me,
With spinning leaves,
Down and round,
Hundreds and thousands,
Plunging to the ground.
Leaves, brown and gold,
Crispy and old.
Rows of flower beds,
Staring at flowers,
Lowering my head.

Kirsty Greenwood (11)
Windmill Ridge Middle School

AUTUMN

Golden leaves,
Crunching, crunching,
Children playing, kicking
The golden, golden leaves.
The sky is golden,
Time is passing.

Golden leaves,
Floating in the wind,
Children playing in the golden leaves,
Crunching, crunching.
The sky is golden,
Time is passing.

Ben White (11)
Windmill Ridge Middle School